Doing Your Own School

The Great Atlantic and Pacific School Conspiracy

Steve Arons	Walt Senterfitt
Alice Milmed	David Steinberg
Pam Senterfitt	Dorothy Stoneman

Royalties from the sale of this book will go in part for support of The Learning Place, a free junior and senior high school in San Francisco, and The Group School, a working-class high school in Cambridge, Mass.

Doing Your Own School

A Practical Guide
to Starting and Operating
a Community School

by The Great
Atlantic and Pacific
School Conspiracy

Contents

About This Book

The six people who wrote this book came together with experiences at three schools, The Learning Place, The Group School, and The East Harlem Block Schools. The book is our attempt to collect and put in a useful form not only our own experiences but those of people working in many other new schools. While we six members of an imaginary conspiracy collectively wrote these pages, the work is really a product of the new school movement.

We started by contacting over a dozen new schools which seemed to us to represent different educational ideas and social values, run by people who are serious about their work and would be serious about their differences. You will find references to these schools throughout the book, and a brief description of each school at the end. We asked friends at each school to write or talk to us about their school, much as they would if they were trying to explain to someone how they had arrived where they are. As we read through the information we received, we noticed a number of common problems and a number of different solutions reached by each group. This became the central theme of our task—describing problems which often occur and telling of the practical solutions different people have reached.

Then began the laborious and entirely unfamiliar task of collective writing—six people trying to write one book together. There were agreements about a table of contents, drafts and redrafts of chapters, collective criticism of each other's work, egos damaged and repaired, and so much cross-editing that we are at a loss to say who really did write which section. The book was written and rewritten three times and between each draft there were very many helpful criticisms from friends and from people at new schools around the country.

Every book has a list of people who helped it to be born. Ours does, too. But in our case these people did so much of the hard, creative work involved that they might be listed as authors. Since they did not go through the head-banging drafting sessions, however, we thought it fairer to acknowledge their help without saddling them with the responsibility for the errors we may have made in putting the book together. We list everyone, including ourselves, with reference to the source of their contribution, in order to give a better idea of what went into making this book.

Mrs. Inez Andrey, former director, Martin Luther King School, San Francisco, Cal.

Judy Areen, Center for Study of Public Policy, Cambridge, Mass.

Nancy Arons, head teacher, Simmons Child Study Center, Boston, Mass.

Stephen Arons, teacher, The Group School, Cambridge, Mass.

John Cawthorne, Education Development Center, Newton, Mass.

Michaela Conger, co-founder and parent, Primary Life School, San Francisco, Cal.

Neil Didriksen, director, The Group School, Cambridge, Mass.

Jane Goldman, teacher, Primary Life School, San Francisco, Cal.

Carolyn Grace, freelance writer, Cambridge, Mass.

Judy Herrick, teacher, Berkeley Montessori School, Berkeley, Cal.

Phyllis Jarmolowich, Chairman, Parent Board, Ironbound Children's Center, Newark, N.J.

Joan Kessler, Michael Community School, Milwaukee, Wisc.

Gary Krane, Berkeley, Cal.

Charles Lawrence, director, Highland Park Free School, Roxbury, Mass.

Alice Milmed, teacher, The Learning Place, San Francisco, Cal.

Tim Parsons, Experimental Schools Project, Newark, N.J.

Tom Roderick, director, Day School, East Harlem Block Schools, New York, N.Y.

Pam Senterfitt, teacher, The Learning Place, San Francisco, Cal.

Walt Senterfitt, teacher, The Learning Place, San Francisco, Cal.

David Steinberg, freelance writer and former teacher, The Learning Place, San Francisco, Cal.

Susan Steinberg, former teacher, The Learning Place, San Francisco, Cal.

Dorothy Stoneman, former director, East Harlem Block Schools, New York, N.Y.

Derek Winens, Ironbound Children's Center, Newark, N.J.

Kathy Woodward, Center for Study of Public Policy, Cambridge, Mass.

We wish to thank the U.S. Office of Economic Opportunity. It was under grant number CG 8542 that part of the work which resulted in this book was done. The grant made it possible for everyone who helped to be fairly compensated for his/her work.

Finally, thanks to Beacon editor Ray Bentley for understanding us and this book. And thank you, Beacon Press, for publishing the Pentagon Papers.

Start at the Beginning

The purpose of this guide is to provide practical help to groups of people who want to start new schools (whether inside or outside the publicly funded system). People who are already working on new schools will also probably find this guide helpful in raising basic questions. We have assumed that our primary audience is parents and community groups, though we have at times addressed ourselves to teachers' groups, students, and even "educators." The focus of the guide is on primary schools, though there are some suggestions for high schools.

Many people begin to think about starting a school of their own because of dissatisfaction with existing public schools. Perhaps you believe your children or those of your community are not learning the basic skills they need to survive and to find a fair share of happiness. Perhaps the children are unhappy at school, or mistreated, or are not feeling confident about themselves and proud of their cultural and historical roots. Maybe you have tried to change the school and become frustrated. Or maybe you just have the feeling that things aren't going to get better soon enough to benefit your kids.

These feelings and experiences are often what are on people's minds when they draw together and utter that first "maybe we're going to have to do it ourselves." This guide was made by many people who are already doing it themselves. We have discovered that bad feelings about past schooling are often replaced by the excitement of working with kids, the strength of doing something for yourself, and the confidence of people who are building a community. The humor, seriousness, curiosity, and delight at learning, of children going to school in a healthy atmosphere cannot help but rub off on adults. The work of starting and running a new school has been energizing and meaningful and possible for many people.

1

There are, of course, plenty of problems waiting for you if you want to start a new school. This guide offers help on the first steps in recognizing and solving these problems, but before you begin reading you should have a sense of what is involved.

You will need to organize people around the idea of starting a school and you will have to arrive at some shared view of what you want out of the school. This means talking to friends in the community, meetings, studying other new schools, and the hard work of reaching an agreement to work together.

You will need to have a way of governing the school and arriving at decisions on which you can build. This means figuring out how much power parents, teachers, community people, and students should have.

You will need to get incorporated, file for a tax exemption, get insurance, and be sure you know all the applicable state and local regulations. This probably means finding a lawyer whom you trust.

You may want to find a director, and you will need to interview and hire teachers and other staff people. This means a lot of looking and many hard judgments about what kind of help you need and what kind of working relationships you want.

You will have to worry about money. This means understanding how to survive without much money and developing ways of increasing your resources without changing basic school values. If you are starting a school within the public system, or taking over an old one, your problem will not be money but administrative and political restrictions. We haven't discussed this subject but it could be a guide in itself.

You will need to enroll students. This means deciding how to define your community, how to be fair to all interested children and parents, and what your attitude is toward students.

You will need a building. This means looking for something that meets your own needs and then dealing with health, fire, and building inspectors.

You will need to develop a curriculum and gather materials. This means taking all your own value judgments and all the expert advice you can get and translating it into a working school.

You will need to get certified by state or local school authorities. Depending on the state you live in this process may be simple or complex. In most places you will need not only a clear sense of purpose, but plenty of political work and a firm notion of your legal rights.

You will need to deal with all the personal problems of people working together and learning together. This means tolerance, support, honesty, and a critical eye for bullshit.

When all those steps have been accomplished, you will just be starting a school. To do all this without losing the sense of what kind of school you are trying to build and what kind of education the kids need will require considerable commitment and long hours. You should be pretty sure that you want to do it before you start.

If you do want to start, this guide should help. It is designed to provide some possible answers to the common problems of starting and maintaining a school and to ask questions we have found are best brought into the open early, even if they cannot be immediately resolved.

People starting schools should be careful not to imagine that there is any *one* correct answer to questions they face. There isn't, and we have tried very hard not to suggest there is. One of the things we have learned in writing this guide, however, is that no learning or writing situation is free of value judgments. In point of fact, one of our main themes here is to encourage you to be aware of your own value judgments and not to shrink from stating them to others and then building a school around the result. You will find some of our biases in these pages but you will find nothing encouraging or condoning invidious discrimination and no instructions on how to show a profit while running a school.

The information contained in this guide was accurate to the best of our ability as of Spring, 1972; but good schools are constantly changing, and it's possible that some of the information we were given will become history next year. If you should contact any of the schools mentioned, you may find it useful to see what kinds of changes have taken place and why. We also must mention, partly for our own protection, that new schools, especially good ones, are swamped with requests for information and help. If all these requests were honored there wouldn't be time left for running the school or raising money to support it. Keep this problem in mind. Also keep in mind when asking someone for help in your project, it's fair to offer some help in exchange.

We hope this guide is helpful to you in getting your school off the ground, keeping it going, or deciding whether you want to start a school at all.

Enjoy yourself.

CHAPTER ONE

Be Clear About Your Goals

Starting a school can seem like an overwhelming task. There seem to be so many difficult issues to think about and resolve. Curriculum, staff, school governance, parental involvement, choosing students, getting accredited, finding a building. It's hard to know where to begin, especially when you're not sure you're really qualified to start a school. After all, we've been taught again and again that a school is a very special institution, an area best left to professionals who have long years of training and experience.

But when we break through the mystique of professionalism, we find the real work is not too hard or too complicated for us to do. And in many cases having these jobs done by non-professionals brings a fresh perspective and cuts through a lot of artificial complication. Many non-professional people who have started new schools have had the refreshing experience of discovering how much they can do themselves. The lesson of these new schools is that if people are ready to work hard and keep working as real difficulties arise, there's no reason why a group of "untrained" people—parents, inexperienced teachers, even students—can't start and run an excellent school. But where to begin?

Start at the beginning. Why do you want to start a school anyway? What would the ideal school be like for your situation? What do you want your school to accomplish? Broad questions like these are hard to think about concretely, but they are important. How you approach the more specific issues depends on what you're trying to do. If you're not clear on your purpose, all the rest is building on sand. When The Learning Place (a free junior high in San Francisco) was started, those of us who worked there found all sorts of new possibilities we had never even thought about when we were in school. It's so easy to limit yourself to making minor changes in familiar school models you see; but in starting a school, the sky's the limit. You may decide you want to stick fairly close to traditional models, but at least you have the choice.

Think about what a school is, down underneath all the particulars of books and class schedules. What does it mean to get an education? How does learning happen? When do people *want* to learn? How does a school help its neighborhood? How does school relate to other institutions in the community and the problems of the future? Public schools generally work off one particular notion of these issues; and you may agree or disagree with their direction. It's entirely up to you. Does a school mean desks in a row? Does it mean classes with one teacher and a bunch of kids? Does it mean classes at all?

As you begin to define your expectations, keep in mind that whatever you plan is likely to change once your school actually starts. In fact, some goals probably won't be clear until you have lived with your school for a while and seen it deal with real problems. It would be possible to set your goals so exactly and narrowly that your school would end up cramped from trying to fit reality into the framework you constructed. The best approach is to work out a clear set of expectations and to think of them flexibly, so you can refine your ideas as the school develops. Think carefully of goals before you start, but don't stop thinking about them after the school begins.

Too many schools think of goals in high-sounding general phrases that don't have much real content. Get under the rhetoric to a real sense of what you want to have happen. Don't feel your goals must be general enough for the whole world to admire; think of what makes sense to you and your community. If your sense of goals is clear, it will help to examine your school as it goes along and judge what's working and what's not.

In thinking about goals, start with the focus that brings your group together. Do you want to do a school based on a particular educational philosophy? A school for children with particular learning problems or abilities? A school focusing on the needs of a particular ethnic group or neighborhood? A school providing religious instruction, or an opportunity for parents to be actively involved in their children's education? All these types of schools have been started successfully somewhere.

Defining Goals

You may have a vague sense of what you want your school to be, but find it hard to pin down very exactly. You may find that different people involved in starting your school have different ideas about what it should be trying to do, or differing priorities among their various goals.

The people who started the Ironbound Community School (Newark, N.J.) dealt with these problems by organizing a series of seminars in which parents talked out the basic educational issues. The seminars met once a week for ten weeks, for two hours in the evening. Parents had a chance to discuss what they wanted, to have visiting experts advise on various issues, to visit other schools, see films, and evaluate new learning materials. Parents looked at the problems their children were having in school. They discussed their relationships with their children, including how their children were disciplined and how they learned. They recalled their own educational experience and how inadequate it was. They heard a speaker talk about using "open classrooms" as a specific educational technique. Out of all these discussions the parents found they gained a clearer sense of what they wanted for their children, and of how to begin moving to implement what they wanted. The goals of the school emerged directly from the seminars, and the process of meeting together over a period of time forged a cohesive group with a common sense of purpose.

Arriving at a common sense of purpose is not necessarily an easy process, and you should expect conflicts and difficulties. Discussions and meetings may not be the best way for you to arrive at your goals. Often people need to work on specific projects to understand their goals and motives clearly. Don't be afraid to begin some modest tasks as a way of understanding goals after thinking and talking and visiting have taken you as far as they can. The Group School (a working-class high school in Cambridge, Mass.) started with a wide variety of purposes and interests, not apparent to everyone. The school moved through a slow and painful process of setting up a part-time school. It required a great deal of energy, but in the process of working through these difficulties, the people produced an organization with a strong consensus around a limited set of goals. By the time the full-time school came into existence, the Group members had worked together closely enough to know themselves and the expectations of others pretty well.

The process used for defining goals by a small group of teachers may be different from the process used by a group of parents, and both may be different from a diverse group of students, teachers, and parents. Whatever process you follow for defining goals, however, you will do well to face disagreements early, rather than gloss over them with superficial language, only to have them reappear in more virulent form once your school begins. You may find the differences you uncover make it impossible to work together as a group. Michael Community School (an elementary community school in Milwaukee) found a division between parents who wanted predominantly Catholic education and parents who wanted to move away from a parochial context. Berkeley High Community School found the same division between people emphasizing political action and those emphasizing a particular educational philosophy. If such a division exists in your group, you will want to know about it early, so you can form two separate schools if necessary rather than spend all your energy fighting for control of a school that makes no one happy.

Some Goals

Some different kinds of goals of existing new schools are presented below. They reflect different issues schools have considered important. Not all will be relevant to you and your school, but some probably will be. We discuss these issues in the hope that specific examples will help you clarify your own goals.

Basic Skills. The most familiar goals for a school are those that focus on how much and what its students learn. We see this emphasized in the public schools through tests of reading levels and mathematical abilities. While many new schools seem to move away from this quantitative way of evaluating themselves, most have retained these specific learning goals for their students. The parents who formed the East Harlem Block Schools, for example, made it clear that they wanted their children to make definite progress in reading, writing, and math. The students here came primarily from Spanish-speaking families, and their parents were concerned that they become skilled in reading and writing English, while retaining their Spanish. With students who had difficulty in these areas, or who expressed little interest in these subjects, the parents expected the teachers to work extra hard to generate that interest.

Other schools also set specific learning goals, but in less traditional areas. A school focusing on the needs and interests of Black students might want to stress a Black studies curriculum or one based on the political and economic needs of the Black community. In another instance, ecology and natural sciences might be stressed, or particular job skills, or knowledge of how to use the political process. Your view of what kinds of knowledge it takes to survive in the world may determine your specific learning goals.

Some schools, less concerned about the specific knowledge or subject matter, focus on a variety of characteristics they would like to see their students develop. Berkeley Montessori School, for example, emphasizes that its students learn to use all their senses in discovering the world around them, that they learn to take care of themselves and their environment. San Francisco School wants its teachers to foster student independence, so that individual students will be able to follow their curiosity and discover what is important to them. Both these schools are concerned that students not fall into patterns of simply doing what they are told by adult authorities. They want their students to learn to define their own interests and activities, to become self-motivated learners. The East Harlem Block Schools put it this way: "This kind of sensitivity is necessary for . . . giving the children the power they will need to forge the alternatives which mean personal freedom for themselves and their people."

The goals of some schools reflect a basic concern for personal growth among students. Presidio Hill School in San Francisco works to give its students a positive sense of themselves and at the same time to have them appreciate the differences, the uniqueness, the contribution of others. Related to this is the goal of "breaking down stereotypes of all kinds: race, sex, age, ethnic, socio-economic, or whatever." The Learning Place makes its personal growth goals more specific in the following list: "Learning to make decisions for yourself, learning to evaluate your own work, learning how to work in cooperation with others and how to work alone, finding and evaluating other people's information as a step toward reaching your own conclusions, coming to grips with what it means to be a man or a woman, becoming aware of your strengths and weaknesses, understanding and expressing your emotions on a variety of levels, and developing rich relationships with other individuals."

The age of the student you intend to enroll may influence appropriate goals. As students get older you may want to help them figure out the direction they want to move in over the next few years, and help them to be able to set up an educational program that facilitates this growth. This involves students assuming responsibility for their own lives, allowing students to choose their own educational programs, and encouraging participation in the governance of the school.

The Learning Process. Schools often set goals about *how* learning should come about, emphasizing the personal and teaching relationships in the school. These goals are particularly important to people who have started schools in order to practice a particular educational philosophy; but people starting schools for other reasons have also been concerned about process and the feel of their school.

A common theme among new schools emphasizes students' learning by being free to choose their interests and to follow them through. The concern here is that students be able to pursue their unique interests, with the teacher helping them as they define what they want to do. According to one school, a teacher may help students move on their own interests and may suggest work, but may not play so active a role as to "interfere with the child's interest in learning" or his curiosity. A similar process concern among the East Harlem Block schools was that their children enjoy their school, get along well with teachers, and be treated with kindness and respect. Some of these schools have been surprised by how well students learn even the academic subjects in this atmosphere.

Many schools seek to substitute cooperation for competition in learning. They strive to build a feeling of community, of mutual acceptance and trust that includes both teachers and students. To accomplish this a school may use frequent school meetings, encounter groups, rap sessions, camping trips, and learning marathons, as well as reducing student competition in the classroom. Identities as staff people and students may be de-emphasized so people can be more like members of a learning community where each individual is respected and where people learn from each other. The New Community School (Oakland, Cal.) has a motto that "teachers teach students, students teach teachers, and students teach each other."

The Learning Place sets the goal of having its learning process include as much encounter of new and unfamiliar areas as possible. The school accepts failure as part of the process, and does not try to avoid failure. Students are encouraged to try new areas and activities, even if they're not sure they will be able to succeed. Working with students to overcome fear of failure supports this process of exploration.

How learning takes place at your school will depend on *what* your students are trying to learn. To complete the circle, the process you establish for learning will, in turn, influence what subjects or skills your students explore. Because of this close interrelationship, it's important that your skill goals and process goals harmonize well. You may think there will be a conflict between learning and process goals. For example, you may want children to learn math but also enjoy themselves and follow their own curiosity. Ironbound Community School was able to harmonize these goals because it found that when it allowed students to roam anywhere in the building and pursue interests, this natural pursuit resulted in learning even the standard subjects.

Teachers and Parents. Although students usually receive most consideration in thinking about goals, it's good to remember that teachers and parents are also important and to consider what your school will do for them. This is dealt with in more detail in sections about staff and parents, but we mention it here because you should think about teachers and parents as you formulate more general goals. The kind of work teachers feel comfortable with, the degree of support and criticism they need, and the best atmosphere for them to be comfortable should be discussed. So too with the parents. How parents relate to teachers, what roles parents want to play and should play according to the school's goals, what parents get out of being part of the school, and how much the school relies on parents for its existence are all important in defining your goals. All people in your school community will have needs to be met by participating in that community.

Community Development. Schools are often begun by people in a specific neighborhood and grow as an expression of the life and interests of that community. For these schools, goals that go beyond the traditional are often important. Perhaps your vision of a school is not simply as a learning place for children but as a community institution serving many other needs. Perhaps social and personal needs of the school's families are also going to be a part of your program. Day care, health services, family counseling, recreation may all be included. Perhaps, too, you see a community school as one which concerns itself with the social and political issues its community faces. Thus, The Group School specifically sets the goal of relating itself to issues like housing, jobs, unemployment, racism. As a community institution, The Group School is working more explicitly to establish a viable community organization controlled by and responsive to the community in which it exists. The school works to help its students become more aware of community concerns, and to develop skills and discover possibilities for returning to the community in which they have been raised.

Michael Community School (Milwaukee) sees itself fundamentally as a resource to provide varied educational facilities to its entire community. Not only does the school work with students, it also includes many other community functions—adult education, health programs, nutrition information, and community social activities.

The East Harlem Block Schools act as an advocate for the children and their families, educating parents on their health needs and rights —on how to get what they need from local hospitals, for example. A parent coordinator works with parents in welfare centers and with landlords. The school is a focus around which parents can come together and work to have their needs met by the larger society. In the school parents, students, and teachers can work to educate themselves, to bring themselves together, to take effective social action. This point is stressed in the following excerpt from an article by Tom Roderick, of East Harlem Day School:

By way of summary I shall try to distill from these experiences the feelings and thoughts which stand foremost in my mind as I work with children in East Harlem and share with them and their parents the struggle to build a school.

I begin by taking the concerns of the parents very seriously. Their anxieties about the behavior and academic progress of their children in school cannot be dismissed as retrogressive or conservative. Their children are growing up in a ghetto. Black or Puerto Rican and poor, the children have two strikes against them already in a racist society which destroys many and leaves many more virtually powerless. Their struggle is for survival; and above all they need power: personal power, which includes self-esteem, cultural pride, and basic academic skills; and collective power, the faith that through concerted action people can change the institutions which affect their lives. Only with these kinds of strengths will they be able to confront the society and forge the alternatives which mean personal freedom.

The alternative of the street is there already: for some it is a viable path; for most it is not. Our goal at the Day School is to help the children develop other alternatives, so that when they come of age, they have choices, real choices, about the kinds of lives they want to lead. As alternatives open up for them we hope that the children will not grow to reject the street and their cultural background but maintain respect for them while working for change.

This means that we are primarily concerned with developing in the children a sense of hope, of faith in their power to help shape the future. Fostering hope begins with the individual child finding and developing his strengths in the classroom; it leads right into politics: working together to effect change.

To pursue these goals, parents, teachers, and children at the East Harlem Day School are shaping a school which is unique: our school is not patterned on a particular model but represents our attempt to find the most relevant approach to the needs of our particular children and community. What we are coming to shows the influences of Leicestershire and of Schools for the Future. We believe that children learn best from involvement with materials; that the teacher's role is crucial but that children can also learn a great deal on their own and from each other; that children need to have the freedom to move around and talk and relate freely with each other; that the best learning begins with what the children bring but does not stop there; that learning should not be fractured into different subjects offered at different times in a disjointed way but that children should be encouraged to develop their interests through projects which integrate different disciplines and modes of expression; and that children should take on a great deal of the responsibility for selecting their activities.

Yet this basic framework is not in itself true freedom and independence. It is only one precondition for freedom. If the choices offered to children are boring, if the child gets no help in seeing the possibilities of the material or activity, then his "freedom" to choose is meaningless. If he chooses, for example, to work in mathematics, but only does teacher-made exercises in a mechanical way, then his freedom is severely curtailed. On the other hand, he is no further ahead if he plays with mathematics materials but gets no guidance from someone who can open up new possibilities for him. The fullest kind of freedom is to be able to learn, discover and do significant creative work on your own.

Social Action. A number of schools see themselves actively involved in a still broader process of social action going beyond the immediate school community. Some see starting a new school as a lever for changing public education in their city. Other schools deal with social conditions explicitly in their curricula or work to influence public and other private schools toward change.

New Community School defines itself as "an educational institution in the movement for social justice." It sees itself as a community taking action on specific issues in the larger community and society. This learning process helps students become aware of the needs of oppressed peoples and the issues involved in their liberation. The school encourages its students, parents, and teachers to move on these issues, to train themselves in new kinds of action, and to evaluate the effectiveness of this action as they go along.

The East Harlem Block Schools have found their community perspective has broadened from a preoccupation with the needs of the local community to an awareness of the schools' relationship with poor communities throughout the country. The schools now try to be responsive to other community groups working to establish similar

schools, and to constantly represent the needs of poor people in negotiations with day care administrations.

The more you clarify your goals, the easier it will be for you to
develop. With a clear basic direction, and a strong sense of common
purpose, you will have a good foundation for dealing with later conflicts. You will be able to refer to your purposes, and avoid the
situation of new people expecting something different from what
you're doing and then being disappointed and resentful.

Once you arrive at a clear sense of common goals, you will have
worked together as a group, gaining a sense of how that feels and the
conflicts it produces. You will have a sense of being a close-knit group
of people doing something together.

What's left is to translate your goals into the reality of a working
school.

CHAPTER TWO

Governing Your School

Who will make the decisions in a new school?
Who will decide the general direction, the educational philosophy,
    the administrative structure and procedure?
Who will make the many day-to-day practical decisions?
Who will hire and fire teachers and administrators?
Who will ultimately resolve conflicts?

The purposes of the school will influence how these questions will be answered. If your purpose is to be a parent cooperative, obviously you will want parents to have the ultimate authority, and the formal structure would reflect that. Public schools are considered to serve the interests of the entire city or district, and thus their governing boards are usually elected by vote of all registered voters, whether or not they are parents. Many established private schools have self-perpetuating governing boards, composed perhaps of parents, former parents, and non-affiliated individuals who have an interest in the school. Some new schools for junior high and high school students are governed by boards on which students are the majority and staff the minority.

Governing Board and Representation

Most schools have a governing board, frequently called a board of directors, which sets the overall direction and philosophy of the school, makes budgetary and other major financial decisions, and (usually) hires and fires at least the principal or director, and perhaps the teaching staff as well.

In deciding whether to have a board of directors or some other central governing committee, keep in mind the need to have decisions made and not simply discussed and left hanging. Especially in the first year of a new school, the number of basic decisions which must be made can be staggering. Having a process in which your entire community or school is involved may become cumbersome and too slow to really respond to the need to keep the school developing.

On the other hand, it's important to be sure the board is responsible to the community and doesn't get carried away with its own authority. This can cause great dissension, and frustrate efforts to have everyone feel he/she is contributing to the development and governance of the school. One school deals with the problem by publishing all board decisions throughout the school and allowing a majority of the school members (in this case teachers and students) to reverse a board decision at any of the periodic community meetings. This board is also very careful to discuss issues with school members before making decisions—to bring crucial issues directly to the community.

Whatever your decision you should think carefully about the balance of power between school and board. The problem of allocation of power will also arise for the director and staff (see Chapter Six). Frequently there are one or more committees making decisions in particular areas within the general policies of the governing board. For instance, often a personnel committee plays a major role in hiring and firing teachers. Other committees sometimes include budget, curriculum, building, admissions. Committees provide a way of involving more people and perhaps of getting work done faster, but cumbersome committee structures sometimes create more work than they are worth. In this instance, as with others concerning governance, be sure you are creating government needed because of actual work to be done rather than government simply for its own sake.

Who should be represented on the board? The starting point for answering this question might be parents. If you are a group of parents starting a school, you may well want the board to be entirely parents. Even if you are a group of teachers or other citizens, you may consider that parents—especially of young children—should have the ultimate authority over their children's education.

If you are planning a community school, there may be other

interests you want represented, such as outstanding community leaders who are not going to have children in your school. Or you may wish to have an all-community election of board members of your school. Some community schools have run into the problem that more experienced parents or community leaders—often those with middle-class backgrounds—tend to dominate board and committee discussions and decisions. If part of the community school's goal is to involve those parents previously most excluded from participation in their children's education, it may decide to limit the board to low-income parents or stipulate that the board and its committees must have a large majority of low-income members.

If a goal of your school is to have a racial and ethnic balance or diversity in the student body, you will want to make sure that the board reflects the same balance and diversity.

What about teachers and staff? Are they to be regarded primarily as employees and advisors or as partners in the whole educational process with some interests of their own that deserve to be represented on the board? Frequently, community or parent-cooperative schools serving low-income parents inexperienced in organizations want to make sure that professional educators do not dominate decisionmaking. They often decide that the board should be all parents, with the staff in an advisory capacity, though obviously respected and relied upon.

You may decide that the teachers have a legitimate interest in helping shape the school along with parents and students and so should be formally represented on the board. This most commonly happens when the school is started by a group of teachers or a group of parents, students, and teachers together.

The question of board membership is closely related to the way you define the school community. You must consider not only who will be on the board, but who will be allowed to vote for board nominees. You might, for example, have only parents on the board, but allow teachers to vote in elections along with parents. The subject of defining the school community is dealt with in Chapter Four.

Students and Decisionmaking—Who Is Running This Place?

Some important questions to consider include, "How much distinction is there to be between students and teachers?" "What kinds of responsibilities should students have?" "How much are the teachers willing to trust the judgment of the students?"

Existing schools involve students in school governance to widely varying degrees. Elementary and pre-schools naturally delegate little decisionmaking responsibility to the kids. Many new junior high and high schools involve students intimately in school functioning.

At both The Group School and New Community School (Oakland, Cal.), students participate in setting basic school policy. New Community School states explicitly that:

> "Students are on the Board of Directors and school committees so they will be in positions where they can lead, where their views can make a difference in how the school operates and what it does. The actuality of the school should be shaped as much by the students as by the staff."

Schools have found they can derive important benefits from involving students in this area. Taking part in decisionmaking often helps students become responsible for themselves and aware of the personal difficulty in applying group standards to people with different views. In sharing responsibility with students, adults also reduce the likelihood of misinterpreting student opinions and making decisions that breed student dissatisfaction. In addition, if adults handle all governance and policymaking, children are more likely to view them with the awe, distrust, and fear they sometimes assign to authorities.

Although it's definitely possible to structure a school to include student involvement on these levels, it's not easy for students or staff to become accustomed to this degree of sharing responsibility. For example, student say in handling finances at The Learning Place involved deciding whether money would be allotted for staff medical insurance coverage. It's necessary to consider situations like these and determine whether staff members are willing to accept the possible personal consequences. In most cases students seem to be careful in carrying out their responsibilities and making decisions for their community. In the health-plan discussion, careful consideration resulted in the community decision that it was necessary for the teachers' coverage to be paid by the school.

The fact that student decisions usually agree with those of the staff does not necessarily mean that students handle these unusual responsibilities with ease. When students are suddenly given administrative power, they often find the burden of responsibility too great and resort to trying to please the teachers by guessing what the teachers' response would be and acting accordingly.

While it seems desirable to involve students where possible, both students and adults have trouble accepting this concept. Schools have arrived at several methods of dealing with this difficulty. Each measure is only a partial answer and will be most effective when used with the others.

The Group School has tried to handle student insecurities in decisionmaking by clarifying, redefining, and limiting particular responsibilities to make them more manageable. Students can more easily accept responsibility when they do not feel the entire burden of leadership has descended on them. Along with this measure should come an understanding that more responsibilities will follow as the student community feels more comfortable and able to accept them. Progressive, gradual increase of power is also less threatening than immediate total sharing of the burden. Finally, staff support should accompany student decisionmaking from the start. Teachers must look for students' insecurities at every step and discuss them with students, stressing that these insecurities are shared by adults—because they are.

Involving and Training Parents

If you have decided you want parents to play a major role in running your school, you are going to have to help them overcome a good deal of initial reluctance, inexperience, and even fear. You will be asking parents to do something they more than likely have never done before. They, like most of us, have been conditioned to believe that only professional educators know what's the right kind of education for their children. At first many will still believe they don't know enough and can't learn enough to make wise decisions about educational and administrative matters. Besides, many parents will be new to things like boards of directors, budgets, hiring staff, and the other organizational processes and procedures in running a school. Overcoming negative conditioning and inexperience will be gradual, but here are some hints drawn from the experience of other schools; and you can probably think of more yourself:

1. Run seminars or workshops for all interested parents so they can become familiar with the educational and administrative issues and choices involved in setting up the school. As the school gets closer to actual operation, run more specific training workshops in the different skills parents will need to know. Board members may want training, for example, in conducting meetings, group process, asking questions of professionals, getting information needed for decisions. Personnel committee members may want special training in reviewing applicants' qualifications, conducting interviews, investigating previous experience. All parents should be invited to workshops in the curriculum the school adopts, so they can become familiar with what their children will be learning and how they can help them at home. In general, continuing in-service training of parents is as important as in-service training of teachers and other school staff.

2. Have the staff go out of their way to present issues to parents and make the parents decide on them before proceeding to other business. One technique is for the staff to stimulate vigorous reaction and consideration by aggressively presenting a proposal they know parents will oppose. This method is an honest one, of course, only if the staff makes it quite clear they intend to follow the parents' decision even if it is directly opposed to the staff proposal.

3. Set up one or more staff positions of parent coordinator, to be filled by a parent, with the responsibility of involving other parents in the school by home visits, small group meetings, helping board and committee members prepare for meetings so they feel good about their role in them, helping teachers make parents feel welcome in the classroom and conferences, etc.

4. Employ parents as assistant teachers, community teachers, home workers, and in whatever other positions they can fill now or be trained for. They will immediately contribute a strong parent and community perspective to the school that will help make other parents feel welcome and feel like it's their school. As they become more confident in their positions, and as they learn more about teaching, they can help explain everything about school to new parents and help them gradually feel competent to participate. Also, simply by holding positions of responsibility in the school, they serve as positive models for new parents.

5. Try to see that experienced, articulate parents and staff do not dominate meetings and discussions to the exclusion of less confident, newer parents. This can be a special problem with low-income parents who have not had much, if any, previous experience as participating members of organizations. One school moved to counteract this problem by providing that at least 75 percent of all board and committee slots had to be filled by low-income parents. Another school tried to reduce staff domination of discussions by providing that staff members not attend regular board meetings unless specifically requested to do so by the board.

Day-to-Day Decisionmaking

Once you have a process established for making broad decisions, you need to think about how they are going to be carried out and how all large and small operational decisions are going to be made. It's good to think clearly about several things:

1. Some person or group should be clearly responsible for each kind of decision necessary to run the school. One of the most frustrating things about large schools and school systems is the fuzziness in responsibility; individuals are always passing the buck and sending complainers on a runaround. This can happen also in smaller, alternative schools, either because of insufficient planning or well-meaning attempts to share authority and keep any one person or group from dominating.

2. Make sure that individuals with responsibilities in certain areas are free to make reasonable decisions on their own to carry out these responsibilities. But at the same time you don't want teachers or administrators making what are actually policy decisions in the guise of day-to-day operational decisions. For example, sometimes a problem will come up which the school has never faced before in the same way. Suppose the issue is whether or not to admit a student with special emotional and learning difficulties. Suppose that normally the director is empowered by the board to admit students within the standards approved by the board. If the director were to decide by himself in this case, it might become a precedent that would eventually significantly change the nature of the student body without any careful discussion and deliberation by the board. Perhaps the general rule should be that both staff and board should always examine day-to-day decisions for issues that have not yet been thought out and decided by the board, or other appropriate decisionmaking bodies.

A similar problem arises when the director or a staff member has a particular kind of skill or expertise that no one else possesses. Sometimes such a person makes policy decisions by himself in the process of exercising that expertise. For example, suppose a staff member is expert at writing funding proposals and negotiating with foundations or other government agencies for funding. In the process of negotiations, situations frequently arise when the agency will not agree to fund exactly what the school wants, but will give money for a different program or the original one with certain changes. Should the school agree? Obviously, in most cases the decision should lie with the board or with some other group representing the school's constituency. But many times the habit of respecting a professional's expertise will lead to letting him/her decide since only he/she understands the technical points involved and can judge what the funding agency will actually agree to.

One structural means some parent-controlled schools use in dealing with this danger is to provide that each professional educator in the school, from directors to teachers, works all the time as part of a team including parent paraprofessional staff members or board members. The East Harlem Block Schools provide that some board members can also be parent staff, so there is a link between the parent members of staff teams and board decisions. It works well in both directions; parent staff know what the board decided and what its general thinking is and can remind professional staff whenever necessary. They can also take back to the board an intimate knowledge of day-to-day work and decisions of the school.

Balancing Individual Rights with School Needs

Until the last couple of generations, individual educators had very few rights in the structure of American education. A serious, competent teacher could be fired with no recourse if some parent came to hold a personal grudge or if a school board member's daughter needed a teaching job, or if he/she expressed unpopular views. As school systems became consolidated and bureaucratized, and as teachers banded together to fight for rights and protection, the balance swung in the opposite direction. Tenure is granted teachers and administrators after a very short time and with little or no real evaluation of their competence and dedication. Afterwards, it's difficult to remove teachers even when they are clearly incompetent, uncooperative, or insensitive to the cultures and lives of their students.

New schools must wrestle with this dilemma and find some middle ground that feels right to both staff and parents (or students or the community at large). If you decide to offer tenure to teachers, you should think through what length of service and what kind of evaluation is appropriate before it is granted. Furthermore, you should think about fair procedures for challenging and removing even a tenured teacher if that should become necessary. Many schools have decided against giving tenure, and only have contracts which must be renewed at the end of each year. Some schools also provide a probationary period for new teachers at the beginning of each year, during which they could be removed with cause without receiving the remainder of their year's salary.

In cases where an individual staff member's effectiveness is questioned, it's very important to have a process for decision known in advance and accepted as fair by both parents and teachers. The real key to whether it works depends on the trust among all members of the school community—a trust built gradually and tested in a series of actual problems and crises.

The same difficulty may arise in cases of possible expulsion or transfer of students. Suspension and expulsion have been so abused by public schools that your school may wish to adopt a blanket policy that there will be no expulsions for any reason. On the other hand, instances may arise when it becomes clear that your school is simply not capable of educating a particular child. Providing the school commits itself to finding another place where the child can be happier and better educated, and providing the process for doing this seems fair and sensitive to the family involved, it may be in the school's and the family's best interest to allow the child to leave.

Size and Centralization

Most people realize that a key problem of the public school systems is sheer size, both of individual units and the entire system. If you are seriously interested in a participatory form of school governance and a non-bureaucratic form of learning, the question of size is important. In a very small school—50 or fewer students—it's not too difficult for everyone to participate. In general school meetings everyone can ask questions and make suggestions. But the larger the school, the more difficult participation becomes. It's very easy to have good formal democracy, a board elected by all the parents, for example. But if this is the only or main means of participation, most parents are going to be excluded or represented only indirectly. They still have the power of raising hell if they don't like what's going on, and with a parent board the chances are their complaints will be sympathetically heard. But this is really just a negative or veto power. Very few parents are actually involved in planning or deciding what steps to take.

One way of solving the problem is by having a decentralized structure, as the East Harlem Block Schools do. Here, the parents of each classroom elect one member to the board of directors. The "local school committee," comprising not more than three classrooms, makes much of the policy affecting those classrooms and hires and fires teachers in that local unit. One factor contributing to the success of their structure is its slow and careful development. The parents originally founded a day care center, then a kindergarten class, and have since added one elementary grade per year.

Sharing Information

Everyone knows of organizations which are open on paper, but are in fact controlled by a small group or even one person. Frequently this can be traced to the fact that this small group, or an executive director, control the flow of information. Since they know the most, they naturally have the most say in decisions. Even if someone else feels strongly about an issue, he can be neutralized by statements like, "But you don't know all the facts."

It's important to be conscious of how information is shared. Are there regular meetings to share information with different groups of people in the school? Is the board consulted and involved *before* policy alternatives or proposals are presented? Or, if not, are staff proposals presented early enough for the board to have plenty of time to investigate the issues and consider alternatives? Are all board meetings open to all parents and/or students? Are staff meetings open to parents?

We have touched on some of the main issues to think about in planning how your school will be run. The process of incorporating (see Chapter Ten) may be a good first occasion for working on these issues. Obviously, all problems cannot be prevented by having a beautiful structure and set of procedures. Often what goes on in organizations is much different, for better or worse, than what its formal structure implies. So you must also think about how these structures will actually work in practice and what extra steps you must take to make them do what you want them to do.

CHAPTER THREE

Parents

What will it mean to be a parent at your school? Possible parent roles in governing a school have already been discussed in the chapter on governance. Beyond that, what about other roles for parents, roles that are possible in new schools perhaps for the first time?

Starting from your purposes, think about how closely you want parents to be involved, and how important that involvement is to you. Do you want parents to take primary responsibility for some areas? Are there some areas in which parents would not be particularly helpful? If it comes down to a question of limited time and energy, how much time can you spend developing effective parent roles? What are the long-term consequences of not working closely with parents?

When The Learning Place (a junior high) was started, the founders assumed parents should be involved, the more the better, and this involvement would grow naturally from the informal nature of the school. As the school developed, both assumptions proved wrong. It became clear that there were many blocks to parental involvement, that school staff usually put the day-to-day work of the school ahead of working with parents. The staff also found students were opposed to having their parents so closely involved and, further, when the question was raised with parents directly, they agreed with the students.

After the school had been in operation for some time, however, it was found that the political and economic support of parents was essential to the school's survival. Support was difficult to get unless parents identified more with The Learning Place. More important, it was discovered that students had to deal with two very different sets of expectations about their school work—those reflecting the school's standards (heavily influenced by the kids) and those reflecting the standards of each child's parents. If parents and school were to avoid undermining each other, The Learning Place would have to put more energy into familiarizing parents with the school and opening roles for them in the school.

It was awareness of the relationship between school, students, and parents which enabled The Learning Place to shift its position. The lesson seems to be that whatever your decisions on parent involvement, they should be flexible and not based just on assumptions about what *ought* to be.

If you decide you want parents to be closely involved, you can begin to anticipate some of the problems other schools have had and begin looking for ways to overcome them.

Parent-School Distance

One basic problem arises because parents, traditionally, aren't involved in the day-to-day, nine-to-three activity of a school. Consequently, while students and teachers can begin working together closely as a real community, parents have trouble sharing this sense of group work and commitment. Without this shared sense, all other forms of parental involvement tend to be strained and distant. Parents feel uncomfortable relating to the ongoing work community, have only peripheral information on what is happening, and may misunderstand much of the school program. Swamped with the work of doing a school, teachers often become preoccupied with the immediate problems and neglect working with parents. This makes the separation of parents even more acute.

At Presidio Hill School (an elementary school in San Francisco), parents form a majority of the governing board, but their other involvement is limited to organizing fund-raising events and helping with field trips. Basically they are content to have the hired staff be responsible for the school's daily activities. Relations between staff and parents have been strained because of this separation between parent governance and parent involvement. Basic divisions of this sort between policymakers and those implementing policies day-to-day arise from the widely differing responsibilities of the two groups. More parent involvement might reduce tensions by helping staff and parents adopt similar perspectives on the school's problems.

The structural distance separating parents from teachers and students often stems from feelings among both parents and staff that the school should basically be left to the professionals, meaning the staff. Parents often feel they have little to offer a school because they don't have any formal educational training or experience. And staff often reinforce this with their own sense that teachers are the people who know what's best for the school.

Integral Parent Involvement

An important consideration in dealing with the problem of distance is finding ways that parental involvement becomes an *integral* part of the school operation, rather than an appendage grafted onto the school "because it would be nice to have the parents more involved." The latter kind of involvement generally fails because it isn't essential to the school and generates little energy and interest. The most successful roles for parents seem to evolve out of situations like that of the East Harlem Block Schools, where parents are not only employed as regular assistants to the teaching staff, but the staff is accountable to the parents in a very practical way. At the East Harlem Block Schools, 28 out of 50 staff are parents, and 35 parents also serve on various governing committees. Parental involvement includes teaching assistantships, day-to-day school planning, administration, and working as counsellors. Parents are constantly involved in the day-to-day process of the school. They attend all regular meetings of the professional staff. They have enough information to be an integral force in making decisions and working problems through. Their work is not a luxury to the school, it's vital. The school would close if 35 parents could not be found to accept this kind of responsibility.

It should be noted that this program was developed with great effort and energy by both staff and parents. The arrangements involve close working relationships between parents and staff, both in school and out, and a high level of trust. Staff members recognize the importance of parents being involved, and communicate their desire for involvement in their dealings with parents. The energy they put into working with parents far exceeds that of most other schools.

To build parents' confidence and parent-staff relationships, the Block Schools have used guidance groups and personal counselling for staff and parents together, run by a professional mental health consultant. They use home visits and frequent consultations with parents in groups, in addition to the day-to-day school work parents do. They have worked conscientiously in recognizing and overcoming parental feelings of being unskilled, at having little they felt was important to offer. The development of these working relationships has taken much time and work, but it seems necessary in order to have a truly functional form of parent-staff working community. Two basic factors in such a program's success are: staff must be totally committed to working with and for parents; and parents already on staff or governing committees must be totally committed to drawing in more parents.

Helping Parents Become Involved

It's important in working with parents to be sensitive to their anxieties and look for ways to openly encourage participation and build confidence. You may want to set up special meetings where parents talk about what's on their minds in a relaxed, informal atmosphere. You may want to encourage your teachers to work energetically with parents, and build the strongest possible personal relationships in order to help them feel at ease and willing to express their thoughts. You may want to run workshops for staff and parents on educational issues and techniques, so parents can become familiar with the professionals' way of working and language, and vice versa. You may want to have some of the more confident parents work directly with other parents in encouraging their help. If you simply expect parents to speak up and work their way into the school on their own, you will probably be disappointed, even if your school is initially put together by parents. As The Learning Place found, developing parent participation takes real energy. It also requires a structure that forces staff to deal with the parents' concerns, and in some cases yield to their control and direction.

Advantages for Parents

What are the advantages for parents if they become involved? At the East Harlem Block Schools parents have a better understanding of their child's development and educational requirements. There has also been a definite sense of personal satisfaction and achievement from making positive, working contributions to a school instead of being intimidated by the "professional" educators.

In some schools, the benefits are more concrete, involving adult education, family health, and day care. The more parents become integrated into these schools, the more family services develop.

At The Learning Place, a major focus of school activity is helping students become conscious of their feelings about growing up, taking responsibility for themselves, and working through difficulties of becoming men and women. The staff talks with students about their relationships with their families and this leads to working with parents directly.

Staff members have talked with parents at length about family relationships and in some cases have made real progress in helping to resolve difficult situations. Groups of parents have been brought together to talk with each other about problems they feel in their families. It's possible to go further and develop a parent counseling program on a regular basis, though it's not an easy task and should not be attempted until you have some experience working with difficult family situations.

The close relationship between teachers and students not possible in public school allows teachers to provide outside perspectives to both parents and students. Doing it is difficult—parents may be reluctant to have outsiders "meddle in family affairs." But if you can create an atmosphere of mutual trust, the results can be exciting for everyone involved, and contribute to closer parent relationships with the school in other areas as well.

It's well to remember that it's difficult for a parent to be confronted with a personal assessment of his/her child or the family situation. The problem of trust, privacy, and protectiveness, and sometimes defensiveness, should be discussed openly with groups of parents. Perhaps in such group discussion suggestions can be made about how to respect and discuss different staff and parent opinions about a child without having the situation viewed as criticism or unwanted meddling. Then private conferences can take place based on these suggested methods.

Parental Support at Home

One parent role that is of vital importance, though not related to direct involvement in the school, is providing active support for students when they are at home. In a new school, students have to adjust to new expectations of them and to a new school environment. This is particularly true if the school you start differs radically from traditional schools. The adjustment isn't easy for teachers and parents, and it's certainly not any easier for students. The first months of a new school are marked by the turmoil of this adjustment, as students and teachers together work out new forms of relationships and build a whole new structure of personal interaction.

If parents are not supportive of what is being built at the new school, the student finds himself torn between school and home. Perhaps a new set of expectations is forming at the school, but his parents' expectations are still associated with previous schools. In addition to his own uncertainties about the new situation, he must deal with parental pressure. The results can be disastrous.

It's vital, therefore, that parents actively and energetically support the experimentation their children are doing by being part of a new school. To make this possible, it's important that staff clearly explain what's happening at school, particularly the new and unfamiliar. Staff should watch for questions and misgivings that parents may be reluctant to verbalize, and work with parents to achieve a shared set of expectations for the students. In many schools, staff members are content if parents leave them alone and keep quiet about their doubts. But this is hardly sufficient for a student having trouble with new forms of learning. The difference between active parental support and passive, reluctant acceptance of something not fully understood can make the difference between success and failure of a school with a specific student, or even the success or failure of the school as a whole. The support you will generate from working for a true sense of common understanding with parents will also go beyond the immediate effect on students to help avoid parent-staff conflicts in later situations.

CHAPTER FOUR

School Membership

Defining Community of Interests
or Community of Neighbors

The usual starting point in determining the make-up of the student body is choosing between a school serving a particular geographic community (a defined neighborhood) and a school serving people with common interests (arts, ecology) or sharing certain characteristics (Spanish speaking).

Many existing schools require residence in a particular community or general area. For example, Michael Community School and New Community School serve a particular geographical area and attempt to reflect the racial and economic aspects of the community. The Group School has a different focus; it's designed mainly for students from a white working-class area. It originated to ". . . consist predominantly of students from working-class and low-income families . . . both black and white."

Other schools serve only certain kinds of children. At the East Harlem Block Schools, for example, most of the children come from poor families; district lines for the school were originally drawn to include only tenement buildings. Your school might also be based primarily on the arts or might be weighted heavily toward a science curriculum. It may have a defined curriculum method, such as Montessori, or it may be most interested in children with perceptual handicaps. The list of "specialties" is endless, but in each case the prospective student body is probably not limited to a small neighborhood.

Perhaps the most important advantage of using a geographical community base is that it allows the school to become a broadly functioning part of the community. Parent participation is facilitated when they have ordinary daily contact with one another on the block or in the neighborhood. Cooperative relationships with other institutions (clinics, service agencies, government) may be easier to establish, problems to which the school must relate (outside the classroom) are easier to identify, and the school itself may become a cohesive force in the neighborhood. Problems of governance may be different for schools not based on neighborhood. In thinking about how to define your school community you should keep these governance problems in mind, along with consideration of how you want your school to relate to its neighborhood and what skills and facilities you will need for the group you have made a commitment to.

Balances to Consider

In addition to the question of whether to serve a particular neighborhood, other factors should be examined which may further narrow your target. For instance, you may wish to maintain certain ratios or balances in your student population. The following examples, questions, and comments are intended only as a helpful starting point:

Sexual Balance. How important is a balance of boys and girls? To adolescents, who spend so much of their energy coming to terms with their sexuality, the balance is probably most crucial. To younger children, it's probably not so necessary, though it might be preferable if you're trying to avoid stereotyping sex roles. This balance should also be considered in picking staff.

Age Balance. How wide an age range is desirable? Are there certain ages which should not be mixed? How will the stage of emotional development characteristic of a particular age group affect personal interaction and the curriculum of the whole school? How does the size of your school affect the age range possible?

Even if you have already determined the general educational ideals on which the school will be based, the range of activities and needs of the students will be drastically different depending on their ages. If enough space and staff are available, different ages can coexist. In a more tightly knit group, more conflicts might arise. For example, the Primary Life School feels there are so many changes between the ages of seven and eight that the two ages should be separated if possible. Before deciding on age groupings you might discuss the emotional characteristics and mental development of different age groups with someone knowledgeable about the subject.

Teacher-Student Ratio. What is the most effective teacher-student ratio for classes and for the school in general? How can the school best balance the need for individual attention and the necessity for longer group interaction? How does the type of structure effect the ratios desired? Many schools which stress individual instruction and personal relationships favor a ratio of about 1:7 or 1:8; those with more structured environments (Montessori, for example) allow for as many as 14 or 15 students per teacher.

Racial Balance. How will the goals of the school affect its racial balance? If part of the curriculum will center on the needs and interests of a particular racial group, the school will mainly attract members of that group. If your intent is to enroll members of a minority group but your curriculum and teaching methods are irrelevant to its needs you will have difficulty attracting students of that group. For example, some minority families feel the free school approach is a luxury proposed and defended by middle-class people who have trouble in beoming integrated. If you aim at attracting children from a variety of racial and ethnic groups, you will design a program that stresses racial interaction and is relevant to all groups. (Multi-Culture Institute of Berkeley designed its program with this purpose in mind.)

Emotionally Disturbed Children. Often schools exclude children they do not want to deal with, sometimes by labelling them "emotionally disturbed" even if they're not. Nevertheless, some children do have emotional needs so strong their membership in the school would require basic restructuring of the entire school community or resources you do not have. Your school might actually be destructive to a child who needs special attention you cannot give him. In addition, other school members might become frustrated by fruitless attempts to aid the disturbed child. How much emotional imbalance can the school handle without destroying itself? How can you balance your desire to help people who might fail elsewhere with the disintegrating effects of too much emotional imbalance?

Recruitment and Selection of Students

Some schools have little trouble recruiting students, especially when they develop as split-off or replacement schools for already existing institutions. In one instance, dissatisfied parents who had already formed their own school committee and had forced the hiring of a teacher of their own choice, formed a new school with this teacher and a parent as co-directors. Similarly, Michael Community School began when St. Michael's School, a parochial school, folded for lack of financial support and was replaced by a community school. The initial enrollment was substantially that of St. Michael's Parish.

More commonly, new schools must give careful attention to recruiting. Most schools rely on word-of-mouth, coverage in news media (newspapers, magazines, and radio), and advertisements of school meetings. Preparing a brochure to be mailed to all prospective parents and students and distributing posters are common helpful methods.

You may be able to arrange speaking engagements about the school. If your school is at all innovative, college classes (especially in schools of education), church groups, and public school classes may be interested in hearing about it. Sometimes these groups will request (or at least permit) students to come along. You might also try combining recruitment with some sort of fund-raising venture or group activity, such as a garage or bake sale, potluck picnic, fair, or neighborhood campaign.

In all types of advertising, keep in mind who would be most interested in your school. Give extensive and explicit information about the school's expectations, goals, and methods. This will minimize wasted time for you and parents or students confused about what they are getting into. Your advertising and brochure should stress what you aim to do, not what you're reacting against or trying to avoid.

Many schools have successfully used conferences with prospective families to explain the school and determine whether the family feels comfortable with it. Even if the child and the school seem to fit together well, both school personnel and prospective family will have a much clearer idea of the realities after speaking with each other. Several different types of conference are possible. A few people from the school (most likely just teachers, but possibly teachers and students or teachers and parents) can meet with the child and his parents. This type of conference can be very informative; parents, teacher, and children might all come away with a clearer view. Often, however, the child lets his parents do all the talking. In this case, it would be advisable to arrange for an additional conference which parents would not attend. Perhaps a meeting could be arranged with several prospective students and staff.

Occasionally it becomes apparent from meeting with a prospective student that the school is simply not the right place for him. In the case of a free school, for example, the child or parent may decide the environment is too unstructured or that the parent wants classes to proceed in a more customary fashion.

It's important in meeting the child and parents to consider the child's relationship to his family and the attitudes of *both* parents and child to the school. The Learning Place receives applications from a considerable number of "skeptical" parents. Often their children have been through several unsuccessful experiences in other schools; the parents contact a new school as a last resort. Sometimes students are able to convince parents to try the school, even though they have strong reservations about it. Moreover, parents may show interest in a school because it's the thing to do, or they are being pressured by someone else's opinions. Upon inquiry parents may reveal that they disagree with much of what the school is all about.

If there is a substantial conflict between your views and those of a child's parents, think about whether the child will be able to handle this discrepancy—and whether you can handle it. If many parents differ with you, you'll either have to educate them or yield to their preferences. If these conflicts are not resolved, the parents may undermine the progress of the child or the school may seriously damage the relationship between child and parent.

Being on the lookout for these kinds of potential conflicts is always to the school's advantage. Pointing out conflicts to students and parents may lead them to a fuller understanding of the school and avoid parents having unwarranted expectations about your school.

You may eventually find you have more applicants from your chosen community than places in the school. At this point it's probably most equitable to rely on a first-come, first-served or lottery system of selection. There are many other ways of choosing among applicants who all meet the school's criteria and wish to attend. The presence or absence of other opportunities for the child is one. Whatever method you use, be sure it is clear to parents *before* selection and fair to all concerned.

CHAPTER FIVE

Attitudes Toward Students

Student Involvement in the Learning Process

Learning can be thought of as an interaction among teachers, environment, and students. The element which is central in setting the basic tone of your school will determine your attitude toward the students and the nature of their involvement.

Teacher-centered Learning. Most elementary school classrooms are teacher centered. According to this model, the child does not create his own learning situations. The teacher molds the situation and the student responds. He may express boredom, interest, anger, excitement, frustration, or bewilderment. He finds learning most stimulating when his reactions are taken into account by the teacher.

At Primary Life School the teachers at first presented the children with many choices at once. Students responded with confusion, and chaos ensued. This caused the teachers and parents to reevaluate the environment they had shaped. They reduced the number of choices and introduced new materials more slowly. Student response to the change was encouraging. Children were better able to make choices and focus on particular areas.

East Harlem Block Schools, Michael Community School, Multi-Culture Institute, and Martin Luther King School share this belief in giving ultimate responsibility to the teacher. Each of these schools, however, aims at creating an environment in which the student is treated as an individual. His interests and uniqueness are important indicators to the teacher. The student's responsibility involves making his individuality clear and his preferences apparent. Furthermore, it is the teacher's responsibility to encourage free responses and be sensitive to them.

Environment-centered Learning. In the Montessori-influenced schools, the environment and materials are central. Here the student encounters a carefully ordered world. Montessori materials are programmed, sequential, educational toys similar to those now popularized by toy companies such as Creative Playthings. With their help the child learns to move from the concrete to the abstract, from the known to the unknown, from perceptual to conceptual thinking. He chooses which materials to use and learns by doing. The theory behind this method is that if the child is to have free choice, the materials he uses need to be structured. At many Montessori-type schools the child wanders freely indoors and out, experiencing the world as he wishes and looking to his teachers as guides.

Student-centered Learning. In the third type of model, the student holds the major share of responsibility in deciding what he wants to learn, plays an important part in determining what materials are presented, and takes a hand in molding his own environment. In some situations, students share responsibility for teaching classes. Most schools of this sort have modified the model; responsibility is shared by students and teachers to varying degrees. Teachers may take much or little initiative in preparing materials and shaping school structure. They help students develop their own initiative by establishing an easy, continuing dialogue through which they come more in touch with each student's needs and interests.

Generally, older children are likely to assume more initiative in this way than younger children. Nevertheless, this type of learning situation has been used successfully with elementary school students. Ironbound School (in Newark), for example, believes no hierarchy of responsibility should exist, that everyone should work toward "preservation of interest in learning and the creation of an environment which will stimulate natural curiosity." Students are free to do nothing if they wish. An Ironbound student's experience with building a model airplane demonstrates one way in which learning takes place in this environment. The initial desire of the child was simply to make an airplane. In the process, however, he improved his reading sufficiently to master the instructions while also developing several manual skills.

The Learning Place started by having students take on all responsibility for their learning. Teachers were available at all times and willing to teach classes, but initiated no learning activities themselves. Everyone found this experiment highly unsuccessful. Students and teachers were bored and listless, and little creative learning resulted. After this experiment, the school felt more comfortable about asserting that there is indeed a difference between teachers and students and this difference can be used to make the school environment lively and rewarding. Teachers are aware that students are often turned off because they are afraid to take risks. As facilitators, teachers help students learn by assuring them that risks are necessary and that failure is as valuable to learning as success. Students are still free to choose what to do and not to do, but teachers try to recognize focuses of interest and encourage risk-taking in these areas. Students may ask teachers to help find outside teachers for subjects no one at the school can help them with. Some students may try to teach classes themselves. While some students may choose to do nothing, other students and teachers are also free to try to find out why and to encourage them to become involved. Both teachers and students are responsible in the learning process, and the responsibility is as much one of being honest as it is one of learning and teaching.

These three models are by no means clear-cut; each shares some elements with the others. A flexible teacher-centered environment, for example, allows for considerable student initiative in learning. You will probably find that a conscious blending of methods is most successful. But you should think carefully about the relationship between the kind of learning situations you will use and the attitude toward students you find appropriate.

Setting Limits on Student Conduct

Related to student responsibility in both governance and learning is the question of limits. Who imposes limits on conduct and what are the limits? Some schools impose virtually no limits on students. In others, there are some basic limits, and further questions are handled by teachers. In still others, students, teachers, and sometimes parents pass judgment and impose limits.

At The Group School, the question of settling limits came to a head in 1971 when an attempted robbery by some outside students led to an arrest and the temporary closing of the storefront then used by the school. The school's board of directors (four students and three teachers) responded by allowing only classes and organized activities, eliminating the "drop in" aspects of the storefront. This was then agreed to by the entire school community. Thus, the limit was set by students and teachers together. Greater control was needed to insure survival.

At Berkeley High Community School, students handle questions of individual conduct through student "tribes." New Community School has a steering committee composed of four students (appointed by department heads), one parent, and the department heads themselves (who do not vote). The committee makes most decisions governing day-to-day living in such areas as drugs, class attendance, admissions policy, and conduct.

How much responsibility is to be given to students in this area? In a one-man-one-vote community, students are easily capable of outvoting teachers. If teachers feel very strongly about certain issues, especially those involving the protection of the school or themselves, they must determine whether or not they are comfortable leaving decisions about these matters to the discretion of the entire community. It is also important to remember, however, that the presence of adults can be very powerful even if students formally hold the voting power.

Honesty and openness about the problems of limit-setting are necessary. As in the other areas discussed, delegating responsibility to students may be frustrating to them as well as to teachers. Students may want the security of basic community rules and may want to give much responsibility to teachers. The need for establishing at least some basic limits can be legitimate and important, with both younger and older children. Basic limits can provide a secure structure in which small children can move more easily toward responsibility and independence. Some restrictions on behavior might also serve to eliminate or reduce the bullying which some children find so terrifying and stifling. In addition, the student who annoys or bullies others through his frustration at lack of limits demonstrates his own discomfort at overloading of responsibility. Remember, however, that unjustifiable or arbitrary limits and rules have stifled and frustrated children more often than excessive openness has confused them.

In the case of older students who have been accustomed to rigid limits, the sudden removal of restrictions might be premature. As in questions of governance, these students often reveal their insecurities by doing only what they feel will please their teachers or exactly what they know will not please the teachers. Gradual lessening of limits will probably be more satisfactory to these children.

A community discussion on limit-setting might be advisable. Here teachers must be responsible in discussing honestly their own insecurities about authority.

CHAPTER SIX

Finding the Best Staff for Your School

In selecting and working with staff, you will want to think about:

- How to find the absolutely best staff for your school.
- How to keep the staff accountable to the particular goal and philosophy of your school.
- How to keep the staff feeling good about their work, themselves, and the school.
- How to provide the staff with opportunities to grow as teachers and as people.
- How to reserve for the school the right to fire staff members who don't work out.

How to do all of these things is quite a trick, and deserves a lot of attention. Staff can make or break a school.

Before you can find the best staff for your school, you have to know what you expect your staff to do, so you can match the people to the jobs. Assuming that you know the basic goals and outlines of your school, draw up a list of all the major functions to be performed to make the school work.

Such a list might include:

Children

- teaching and development of curriculum
- admission of new children
- finding psychological services when necessary
- health tests and problems

- finding special out-of-school resources like art programs, athletics, music, dance, science

Family

- planning and running parent programs, educational, social, home visits
- community service referral-welfare, housing, legal, health

Administrative

- business and bookkeeping
- fund raising
- getting a building
- maintenance of building
- over-all coordination
- long-range planning
- liaison with other organizations
- legal and tax work

Staff

- supervision and support for staff
- arranging and planning training programs
- visits to other schools
- arrangements for absences

Having made your *own* list, you will have to decide whether any of the functions demand specialization. That is, can all the functions be divided among a staff of teachers, or will you have to have some additional positions? Will you need a special person for maintenance, or can the whole staff share in keeping up the building? Will you need a special person to work with families, or can your teachers each work with the families of their children? Will you need a special person for bookkeeping? Or can one of the teachers take this on as his particular administrative responsibility while other teachers take on other administrative responsibilities?

The answers to this kind of question depend in part on how large your school will be, the goals you consider most important, and your funds. One school of 120 children has two people working full time on community services for families, and two more people working full time on family health programs. Obviously this reflects some ample funding, as well as a very strong commitment to the families of children in the school. The school did not develop such a family service program until its fourth year. In its first year it had only 35 students, four teachers, and one half-time maintenance man.

You might want to start with the minimum functions that must be performed and the minimum number of positions. You could add jobs and people as you feel the need.

Director

One major question suggested by a list of functions to be performed is whether you will want to have a special person responsible for administration, coordination, and staff supervision. That is, will you want a director? This is partly a question of how you divide responsibilities and whether you think there will be enough administrative or supervisory work to warrant having one person devoted to it.

But it is more than that. It is a question of how you structure the relationships between people in your school. "Director" is a loaded word. So is "administration" and "supervision." These words arouse definite feelings in people.

Your feeling may be that rank, titles, and responsibilities that give some people authority over other people go against the goals and philosophy of your school. You may want a community in which everyone takes full responsibility for the school as a whole, for each other, and for the work to be done. One new school avoids all formal authority relationships among teachers because the school doesn't want to teach the children to regard hierarchy as the natural or desirable state of things.

But perhaps your group believes the elimination of any authority relationships is unrealistic and a poor preparation for the world outside the school. Perhaps instead of continuing authority relationships that usually exist you want to demonstrate to children a new kind of authority and you want to show them that people who haven't usually had power in this society can be in positions of authority. You want the children to have models of people like themselves in charge. At the Highland Park School the head teachers in each class are community people, and the assistant teachers are professionals; in the East Harlem Block Schools the executive director is a community parent.

These two parent-controlled schools have maintained hierarchies, but have reversed the usual power relationships, for a purpose.

In deciding whether you want a director there are some other factors to take into consideration besides philosophy. One is size. The smaller your school, the easier it should be to function without a director. But if you have started small, and have evolved a style of working that doesn't need a director, perhaps you could invent ways of extending that same style to a larger school as you grow.

In addition to size and philosophy, governing structure should also influence your decision. If yours is a staff-run school, in which staff are ultimately accountable to themselves and their own philosophy, they probably do not need a director to keep them accountable to themselves, though they may want a director to help coordinate administrative work. If your school is a parent-controlled or student-controlled or parent-student-teacher controlled school that has a governing board separate from the staff, the board might need a director responsible for implementing its policies and having the authority to hold the rest of the staff accountable to the policies of the governing board. Even if the staff has representatives on the governing board, the over-all policy of the board will not necessarily be a perfect reflection of the over-all feelings of the staff. In that case, it might be helpful to have a person on staff whose job is to implement the board's policies. It may also be helpful to have a director as a bridge between groups in the school, interpreting the interests and needs of all and keeping communications open.

Without a director, a non-staff board of directors could be quite frustrated in its efforts to run a school. How would its policies get implemented? Who would the board hold accountable? How would they track down who is responsible for what? Would they always have to have joint meetings with the whole staff to determine what is going on? If one staff member was not working out, how would the board be expected to find out or take action?

It might also be easier for all the parents if your school has a director. It's helpful for parents to know who to go to with special problems that a teacher so far hasn't solved.

One further consideration is that some teachers might prefer a clear and limited commitment to the school, perhaps because they have other personal commitments. Without a director, you might want all staff members to make the kind of unlimited commitment to the school that a director usually makes. As the school grows, you might be excluding many excellent people from your staff by asking an unlimited commitment from them.

Finally, you should think carefully of how much you need a director in order to be sure that *someone* is making sure that all decisions get carried out and all work gets done. Sometimes work is overlooked or just slips through the cracks if no one is coordinating the efforts. You may wish to have a director for this monitoring purpose but not give him or her power over staff; a director's role can be limited to information, calling meetings to discuss unfinished work, etc., without giving him a position of authority over other people.

If you decide to have a director, you should consider in advance some of the problems that arise out of strong feelings people have about "directors," "administration," and "supervision."

Often both directors and staff members seem to expect that the "director" will know everything and do things beyond everybody else's abilities. This expectation is destructive to both the director and staff. It tends to make the director feel anxious and often inadequate; it tends to make the staff take less initiative, or perhaps become excessively critical of a director who does not emerge as a "leader."

Because people have excessive respect (and fear) of authority, they tend *not* to be honest, direct, relaxed, or open with people called "director," unless the director is particularly skilled at making people comfortable. So staff members often don't give the director the casual feedback and support he or she needs.

Because directors and teachers perform different functions, they may not fully sympathize with each other's problems. Directors may lose touch with what it feels like to be a teacher. They can become preoccupied with how it feels to be a director, with the pressure of their particular responsibility. Since part of their responsibility is for the performance of the teachers, they may become anxious and critical about the teachers' work instead of sympathetic and supportive.

Here are some ideas to help the staff and the director avoid alienation from each other.

• Periodically rotate roles so that the director is again responsible for doing what the teachers do—whether it is classroom teaching or setting up apprenticeship programs. Have the director experience what it is that teachers are struggling with. Of course, if yours is a school where you do not have teachers responsible for particular classrooms, it may be easier for you to arrange overlapping or rotating roles for director and teachers.

· Have a consultant or resource teacher (master teacher) take on some of the responsibilities of staff supervision. Then the resource teacher, having no role in hiring and firing, having no authority in the school, will be the person giving support and feedback to the teachers. The resource teacher is less likely in this case to be anxious and critical than is the director; and the staff is less likely to be paranoid if the person helping them is not their boss. If the director also teaches, he will be subject in his teaching role to the same pressures as the teachers and this will bring them together.

· Have the director involve staff and parents in administrative work to the extent that they are interested or willing (including resource-finding, parent communication, fund-raising, negotiations with outside agencies).

· Define the director's role as clearly as possible. Have discussions during the year of how the director is helping or hindering the staff, what discomforts he feels in his work and whether the expectations of all these people fit reality or not. Keep the problem up front.

Finding a Director

If you want a director, how will you find one? If you have had a consultant you trust he or she can help you by putting out the word with all his/her contacts. Maybe he/she will come up with the perfect person for you. But the chances are you will have to advertise for applicants, and search high and low for a director. You can:

· Put ads in newspapers.

· Notify the placement centers of all schools of education in your vicinity—even outside your vicinity. Graduates of these schools regularly check back when they are looking for work.

· Put notices in education magazines. There are many professional magazines; if you don't know the names, you might consult the librarian in a local college of education.

• Contact teachers' organizations.

As applications come in, you will need an initial screening process. It turns out to be fairly easy to eliminate the majority of applicants on the basis of either their qualifications or their attitudes and personalities. It will save your group time to have two people take responsibility for this initial screening. Short interviews will weed out the impossible applicants.

Applicants should bring you resumés, and should be prepared to supply references. After the initial screening, the next step would be to check references. The best kind of checking can be done by telephone, so you can get a feeling of who is giving you the information and can ask more about the applicant. People will give information over the telephone they would never put in writing. By checking the references you may spot some people who can impress you in an interview but who never come through; or some people who are shy at first, but who do an incredibly good job wherever they work.

Those applicants who pass the initial screening and whose references satisfy you should meet with the entire board (or governing body). You can ask them all the questions you want. You will need to frame your questions in advance to make them as revealing as possible—and to prevent a boring interview. You should also tell the applicants about your own plans and goals. This is very important, since you want to know whether you see eye to eye with your new director.

You may be lucky enough to all agree, deep in your hearts and inside your bones, that one of your applicants is the perfect person to run your school. But don't settle yet. If that person is now teaching or directing in another school, go and observe him or her there. Ask him to act as a resource person or discussion leader in one of your meetings. Or ask him to dinner. Do anything you can think of to see how he functions, to see if he grows on you. You simply can't be careful enough. If you are going to have a director, you need to have one you like and trust.

If your school is starting small, even if you eventually want a director, you might be wise to start the first year without one. You could hire an administrator and the several teachers you need; or you could divide administrative responsibility among the teachers. At the end of the year one of the teachers might emerge as someone you want to trust with more responsibility.

Teachers

Responsibilities

In dividing up functions, you have already decided whether teachers will be expected to carry out administrative responsibilities, or community organizing duties, or other jobs not usually considered part of teaching.

But you need to go further before hiring anybody. As fully as possible, you should define what is expected of teachers. You need a job description.

Strictly speaking, it would be a job description to say, "You are expected to take responsibility for the emotional and intellectual development of 30 children; and you are expected to assume all other kinds of responsibilities that the school needs in the course of developing the school, as determined by the board, the staff group, or the director."

However, such a job description reveals nothing about your goals (except that you want a highly flexible and responsible staff!) and doesn't insure that anything specific will ever be done. It doesn't tell your teachers much about what you really want them to do, and it gives you no basis for holding them accountable for what you want them to do.

It's more helpful to make your job descriptions as specific and clear as possible. It should not be seen as authoritarian to define what is expected of staff. Include in the description:

- your basic goals, especially your views about work with parents, the use of authority and structure in the classroom, and the kind of evaluation you will expect
- the methods you expect teachers to use in reaching those goals
- the role you expect teachers to take in re-defining goals as you go along
- the methods you do *not* want teachers to use
- the miscellaneous work needed from teachers (fund raising, record keeping, administrative jobs, etc.)

If you are sure of your goals but not of your methods, you can tell teachers their responsibilities are to find the best possible ways to achieve those goals. But if you are sure of some of your methods, ask the teachers to use these methods.

For example, a school might say that it expects teachers to maintain good relationships with parents, and leave the method of doing this up to the teacher. But the school might specify in the job description that for the purpose of maintaining good relationships with parents it expects teachers to make two home visits a year, have one parent conference, provide three progress reports, telephone parents about any accident or problem, and learn to speak the family's language.

Suppose you know that you want the children to learn to read, and to enjoy school. You may not know exactly *how* you want your children to learn reading, though you may know you don't want it forced down their throats. In that case, there is nothing wrong with specifying to teachers that they *must* teach reading, that they may choose *whatever method* they consider most suitable, *as long as* it doesn't result in the children disliking the learning process.

In this way, you have stated your goals, you have put some limits on the teachers and defined the area of their freedom. They are not free to ignore reading, and they are not free to make children unhappy, but they are free to use all their skill and ingenuity in attaining two of your school's goals.

If you give teachers this kind of guide, you will avoid a lot of misunderstanding.

Of course, you need not know everything before you start. As you go along you will learn more about what methods will achieve what goals. A good staff will do much of the work in finding out how to attain the school's goals, and they will probably have a role in developing further goals as you go along.

One more word about limits: the question of limits is as important as that of responsibilities. You may know that you do not ever want teachers to hit children, suspend children, curse at children, ridicule children, say critical things about a child's parents in his presence, or insult a child's intelligence. Again, make this very clear to the teachers. Don't assume that the teachers already know—even if they do, the pressures of teaching are very great and teachers sometimes do things they don't believe in. It will help prevent this to let the teachers know from the beginning what you do not want them to do.

Qualifications

Once you have worked out your goals and the specific responsibilities you will give teachers in implementing and elaborating these goals, you are ready to define what qualifications your teachers should have.

Many groups start out feeling that "qualified teachers" means college graduates who have majored in education and are certified by the city or state. That is the state's definition of "qualified teachers." Unless the state law requires it (and you should get some legal advice on this; see Chapter Eleven), you do not need to use anyone else's definition of "qualified." You may have a very different idea of what it takes to be a teacher in your school.

In thinking about qualifications, consider:

- what personal characteristics a teacher will need to be comfortable in the school community you are planning
- what special skills a person will need to contribute something unique and important to the intellectual development of the children
- what special characteristics or skills a teacher will need to support the healthy emotional and social development of the children
- what attitudes the teacher should have
- what kinds of prior experience would be useful
- what kinds of prior training would be helpful
- what kind of people and what *variety* of people you want children to have as adult models in the school

You may not find people who have everything you want. Finding a qualified staff is a matter of balancing what you would like and consider most important with what you can get. But it is helpful to start out with an idea of the perfect people you would like to find.

Balancing your total staff may be important. Some schools end up with a group of highly committed and very nice people who have no experience in teaching or running schools. Try to get a variety of strengths and experience and special abilities among your staff. If you take people with a common weakness you should plan to make up for these common weaknesses yourself by providing adequate training.

Teaching Teams

Many schools have made teaching teams the core of their staffing patterns. Team teaching is a way of making more adults—often with different abilities and styles—available to the children, and a way of having adults share responsibility for a group of children. It makes teaching less lonely, and often brings out the best in all the teachers.

Some schools have teaching teams which include community people or parents along with a "professional" teacher. The reasons: to involve parents deeply in the school process and in their children's education; to create a community in which parents are models for the children; to keep "professional" teachers tuned in and accountable to the viewpoint and experience of parents; to create a total school community which is richer than otherwise possible; to provide parents exciting and satisfying professions; to make a school where children are at home, proud of their own culture, able to speak their own language freely, able to feel continuity between their own childhood and their future as adults.

In deciding how to structure a classroom team, it might be helpful to know that different schools have tried various definitions of the classroom team relationship.

Ironbound Community School has made the team co-equals, to avoid any authority relationship among them and to place equal value on what each will contribute. At Highland Park School a community person is head teacher and a professional is the assistant, specifically to emphasize the contribution of the community person. At East Harlem Block Schools the parent board has put professional teachers in charge of classrooms and parents are assistant teachers. The board wants parents to be head teachers, but it has generally put a strong value on training and educational background of teachers, so the board is providing a high school equivalency course for parent assistants and also paying their way to college.

Relationships between two or three adults working together in a classroom are sensitive and sometimes difficult no matter what the formal relationship is. Different racial or class backgrounds may make it slightly more complex. No matter how you organize, you'll have to pay attention to the team relationships. Since there's no way to avoid some problems, there's no reason not to experiment with what you believe in!

Other Staff

Resource Teacher or Master Teacher. This person is an experienced teacher whose role is to provide support and concrete assistance to other teachers. He or she may have special curriculum knowledge or may just be a very skilled classroom teacher whose personality makes it easy for her to share what she knows in a helpful way with other teachers. The way she gets involved in each class would be defined by her relationship with the teachers in that class and by the needs of the teachers and the class. She may also have other responsibilities, depending on the school's needs.

Parent Coordinator or Family Worker. This person is a particularly trusted and respected parent or community resident whose role is to assist parents and families in any way she can, as well as to draw families into deeper involvement in the school. Involvement with the school is a way to help families—first through the pleasure of involvement—then often leading to employment, training opportunities, concrete help with all kinds of problems. The parent coordinator's knowledge of the family often helps the school understand the child; she is often the person who can bring parents and teachers together for a full discussion of a child's problems.

Personal Counselor. This person may run group counseling sessions or work individually with students whose personal needs require special help.

Consultants. Consultants can be anybody you want in any area you need: curriculum; health; mental health; group dynamics; classroom environment; anything. They can be permanently attached to the school, working perhaps a day or so a week; or they can be called in as needed. Consultants tend to be more expensive than other staff, unless you can find expert volunteers.

Vocational Counselor. This person may be helping high school age kids find jobs, plan to acquire needed skills, and understand the problems of work.

Recruitment and Selection of Staff

You can roughly follow the same procedure for hiring most staff that we described in selecting a director:

- recruiting through advertising, word-of-mouth, schools, appropriate organizations
- preliminary screening through initial interviews and checking of references
- full interview with the hiring committee
- whatever further measures you decide would be helpful: observations, invitations to participate in some of your work, invitations to some social situation, another interview, a meeting with whatever staff you've already hired

Of course, you fully inform applicants of what you believe and what you expect, including the worst! (If you expect not to have any funds for the first three months, warn them!) Let them see the job description and any other statements of goals. Perhaps the applicants don't agree with you, and you might as well find out from the beginning.

If you're hiring the rest of your staff after you've hired the director, of course the director should have a role in the recruiting and selection process. Later on, you might trust your director to do a lot, if not all, of the initial recruiting and screening. But at this point it would be best to work along with the director, sharing the whole process so you can learn as much about each other and from each other as possible. You might make a simple rule that the committee *and* the director will have to agree on new staff members. Schools which consider the relationships among staff members to be crucial might want to somehow involve all staff in the selection.

How to Keep Your Staff Happy

This is all fairly obvious:

- Hire people you like so you'll be nice to them.
- Hire people who will get along with each other.

- Hire people you have reason to believe will be successful. There's nothing like success to make people feel good.
- Give them all the support you can. Don't pull out after they're hired.
- Pay attention to what the staff says they need. Try to give it to them.
- Make sure the school provides ways and times for people to get to know each other, and to enjoy each other.
- Don't work them to death—they need a little private life, too.
- Pay them.
- Give them opportunities to grow.
- Don't keep people too long who don't work out—they drag everybody down.

How to Provide Staff with Opportunities to Grow

Staff Training

Training is essential to the continued growth of the school and its personnel. The type of training is generally the result of the governing body's concern that staff be trained to carry out the stated goals of the school. Thus, for example, the school might require that all teachers share the same training in curriculum methods, group dynamics skills, language, or cultural history. Training may also be arranged after hiring to provide skills the staff has agreed are lacking or to remedy an individual's weaknesses, develop his strengths, or pursue his important interests.

There are many training methods and resources: pre-service training, outside consultants, regular staff seminars, staff teaching each other, outside workshops, college courses, etc. When school and staff or individual agree on the importance of particular training, the school should bear the cost, if possible. And training should be separated from the evaluation process so that growth is not mixed with threat.

Staff Supervision as a Part of Training

Supervision, provided by a sensitive and skilled supervisor or group and accepted by a responsive teacher, is the best kind of training. It relates directly to the specific strengths and weaknesses of each teacher, within his own teaching situation. It should help him solve his specific problems and deepen and strengthen whatever he is already doing well. It should improve his understanding of himself, and of the students he is working with.

The school has an obligation to provide staff with the best possible supervision. Bad supervision is worse than no supervision. Nothing will drive teachers crazy faster than a supervisor who is over-critical, insensitive, and interested in imposing his own concerns on a teacher who is struggling with different issues. On the other hand, nothing will contribute more to good staff morale than a supervisor who is tuned in to the teachers, has real insights and skills to offer, knows how and when to offer them, and who essentially sympathizes with the teachers and likes them.

The following are some mechanisms for supervision:

- The director might regularly observe the work of each staff member; then meet to discuss the observations, make suggestions, respond to the needs of the staff member.

- Periodically the director and staff member might have a comprehensive discussion of the staff member's strong and weak areas with help on how to work on the weak ones.

- Instead of the director providing continual feedback, the school might have a master teacher do it—someone who has little or no involvement in hiring and firing, but whose entire role is giving support and feedback to teachers.

- A school might have a system of mutual support and supervision, wherein teachers regularly observe each other, and meet in groups or pairs to help each other.

- A consultant might also provide individual supervision on a regular basis. The consultant has the advantage of bringing special knowledge to bear on problems teachers are having, with no particular power over teachers. This combination makes it sometimes easier for teachers to accept a consultant's supervision.

As the school gets under way, staff members should have a part in defining what kind of supervision they consider most helpful.

Keeping Staff Accountable to Your Goals and Philosophy

Accountability is essentially an issue of governance. But it bears strongly on the quality of staff work and on staff attitudes. We all know schools in which teachers are held accountable by principals for maintaining law and order and doing paper work. We know schools in which teachers are not held accountable by anybody for what children learn or how they feel.

How will your staff be held accountable, for what will they be accountable, and to whom? Let's start with *to whom?* Theoretically, staff could be accountable to: parents, students, the community, themselves and each other, the government, the director, the people who provide the funds, or some trainers who represent the model teachers are following.

The design of your school will determine to whom the staff is primarily accountable. Obviously, whoever is governing your school is the main group to whom teachers are accountable. Yet you might have a situation in which parents, or students, or teachers were left out of the governing body. And you might want to develop a way teachers could be partly accountable to one of these groups, even though they were not formally represented on the governing board.

Consider a junior high school formally governed by parents, where parents decided that students were old enough to have a role in teacher evaluation. They might:

- put some students on the personnel committee
- ask students for anonymous evaluations of their teachers, to be made available to the teachers and the personnel committee
- set up evaluation classes, in which students are invited to give their honest compliments and criticisms to teachers directly
- give the student body the right to overrule certain decisions of the personnel committee if three-quarters of the students agreed the committee was wrong

· create a student evaluating committee to work separately from the personnel committee but present its thoughts to the teachers and the personnel committee for consideration

When any of these mechanisms are added to the school's structure, the staff becomes more aware of their accountability to students. This would have an important effect on teachers and on the school, especially since in junior high the interests and attitudes of students are beginning to diverge from those of their parents. It would also have an important effect on parents; they would have to give continuous formal recognition to the attitudes of their children.

The point is that formal mechanisms of accountability influence people's attitudes. People tend to take more seriously the feelings, interests, ideas, and needs of people to whom they are accountable. So, make your staff accountable to the people you think the staff should take most seriously. And if there are several groups of people the staff should take seriously, find ways to include them all in mechanisms of accountability.

Once having created an over-all structure of accountability, you have to work out its day-to-day implementation. You'll want both informal and formal mechanisms.

Informal Feedback. If you structure your school as a community of people who like and help each other, there will be many opportunities to get to know each other, develop interest in each other's work, have parties, picnics, workshops, open houses, home visits, shared responsibilities.

Planned Evaluations. Teachers also need some regular and comprehensive evaluation of their work as others see it. Teachers can count on evaluation at regular intervals, know it will be thoughtful and detailed, and will have an opportunity to discuss it and respond.

Firing

Assuming you have provided training, good supervision, and regular planned evaluations for your staff, firing should not be a complicated issue. Staff members who don't work out, despite all the help and support you have given them—who don't make changes requested of them—may be fired.

The firing procedure you follow after supervision, training, and evaluations have failed should include:

- informing the person that firing is a strong possibility and why
- explaining to him how, by whom, and on what basis the final decision will be made
- giving him an opportunity if he chooses to talk with the people making the final decision
- perhaps giving him a final probationary period if there is some new reason to believe he can or will make the necessary changes

Be sure your procedures are clear to all teachers before any issue of firing arises. That way you will avoid much unnecessary anxiety.

Salaries

Your basic range of salaries depends on how much money you expect to have and how much you will have to pay to get the kind of person you want for your school.

Will everyone on your staff get the same pay? Or will you pay more according to need? According to responsibilities? Experience? Training? Think about it before you start. Many groups begin on a conventional salary scale that emphasizes education and responsibility and then find it's difficult to change because they might have to lower some staff salaries.

Some groups have found ways to balance all the factors they value, by starting with a basic pay and adding certain amounts for training, responsibility, need, and experience. Be sure to discuss the possibility of inadequate funds so people are prepared to miss a few checks in an emergency.

CHAPTER SEVEN

Curriculum: Approaches and Models

Many articles and books have been written about curriculum, often confusing and contradictory. One reason for this confusion is that curriculum is often the last area new schools deal with seriously. The struggle for survival of the school itself, and questions of relationship and interaction among the members of the school, are more immediate and sometimes seem to absorb all available energy. Another reason for the confusion is that each school's curriculum is unique, because each community, each faculty, and each group of students is unique.

This section will not provide detailed blueprints for curriculum. A detailed, concrete statement of even one school's curriculum or one type of curriculum would require a whole book by itself. Even if we could do that here, it would be a mistake. You have to make your own curriculum as you go, in accordance with the particular goals of your school, the unique abilities of your staff, and the individual needs of your students. We can give you some starting points and guideposts for your thinking. But remember that at best these are skeletons; you must make the flesh and blood.

Curriculum basically means what you are going to teach and how you are going to teach it. But while you are considering those questions, and maybe even before you start, you must think about what lies underneath. What are the *preconditions* for learning? The most exciting material and teaching methods in the world won't work if the students are hungry, or physically uncomfortable, or afraid of the teachers, or afraid of asking questions, or fighting with each other all the time. Many new schools, in fact, consider eliminating blocks to learning and creating the right preconditions as their most important goal. Thus, the emphasis in preceding sections on freedom and respect for children, involving parents deeply in the educational process, and encouraging warm interaction among staff members and between staff and parents and students. Sometimes these aspects of education are considered under the topic "motivation."

Essential as the preconditions for learning are, it is also essential that a school not stop there. Your job is not done when all the blocks have been removed, and a student is ready to learn. If at that point he is presented with the same boring material or traditional education in the same uninteresting manner, he will quickly turn off again. So you also have to think hard about what is important to teach and how you can most effectively teach each skill, or attitude, or subject area. As we said before, there is no educational cookbook or supermarket or expert to whom you can turn for a ready solution, though you can get help. You must think it out for yourselves, and examine the ideas and experiences of others that seem helpful.

One starting point is to look at a few more or less well-defined curriculum models. Each is based on a set of assumptions about children, how they learn, and what is important for them to learn. Each includes a general approach, and sometimes a specific methodology and set of materials that have been used in many different schools with various modifications. The descriptions which follow are brief and designed to introduce the most important assumptions and characteristics of each model. You'll notice each one includes information about the preconditions for learning as well as points on what and how to teach. If you're interested in pursuing a particular model further, see the bibliography and resources section at the end of this guide.

Curriculum Models

The Open Classroom

The open education approach to primary education is based on a profound and sweeping revolution in English primary schools involving new ways of thinking about how young children learn and about classroom organization, the curriculum, and the role of the teacher.

These new schools are known variously as Leicestershire schools, open structure schools, integrated curriculum schools, or British infant schools. Many innovative community schools in this country have adopted some form of this approach.

Teaching in these schools is based on a definite body of theory stressing individual learning and learning in what has been called the concrete mode—messing around with stuff. The child learns by his own activity; abstract thought is built from layer after layer of direct experience. The theory holds that each child develops at a separate pace and in different ways and that this ought to be reflected in the patterns of teaching. It insists that knowledge does not fall into neatly separate compartments and that work and play are not opposite but complementary.

The theory describes a new role for the teacher as a catalyst and stage manager who provides children with the kinds of experiences which will help them along in their thinking and in learning basic skills like reading and math. The role of the teacher is to create an environment rich in diverse materials for the child to manipulate, then to intervene as a facilitator or guide only to increase the boundaries of the child's exploration of the materials, not to tell him the answers. Teachers work to help the child pursue whatever interests him because these schools have found the child will naturally, happily, and successfully learn the skills he needs. The role of the teacher is to step in and redirect the child when he needs help, not to dominate the child's total time and attention.

Following is a description of the Westfield Infant School for children from five through seven in a working-class neighborhood in Leicestershire, England. Though this example is from England, it resembles classrooms you might find in Morgan Community School in Washington, D.C.; the Underwood School in Newton, Massachusetts; or the East Harlem Block School in New York City.

If you arrive at the school early, you'll find a number of children already inside—reading, writing, painting, playing music, tending pets. Teachers sift in slowly and begin working with students. It's hard to say just when school actually begins because there is very little organized activity for the whole class. You may see a small group of children working on mathematics or reading, but mostly children are on their own. Moving about and talking freely, the children learn a great deal from each other. The teacher also moves about the room, advising on projects, listening to children read, asking questions, giving words, talking, sometimes prodding.

Some open classroom schools have adopted "family" or "vertical" grouping—children of different ages (say five through seven) are mixed together. This further promotes the idea of children teaching children. Family grouping seems particularly successful in the early years, when newcomers are easily absorbed, and older children help teach young ones to clean up and take the first steps in reading. The older children also learn a good deal from playing the role of teacher.

The physical layout of open classrooms is markedly different from most traditional schools. There are no individual desks and no assigned places. Around the room there are different tables for different activities: art, water and sand play, number work. The number tables have all kinds of number lines—strips of paper with numbers marked on them in sequence—on which children learn to count and reason mathematically. There are beads, buttons, odd things to count; weights and balances; dry and liquid measures; and a rich variety of apparatus (both homemade and commercial) for learning basic mathematical concepts.

Every class has a library alcove with books of all kinds available whenever they are wanted. There is a play corner with dolls and furniture for playing house, and often a dress-up corner or a puppet theater.

The teacher leaves much of the day's routine open to the children. The ground rules are that children must clean up when they finish and they must not bother others. There is no special time for separate subjects in the curriculum, and no real difference between work and play. In fact, these schools are based in part on the notion that what adults call play is the principal means of learning in childhood, a notion that seems plausible when you consider how much children learn informally before they come to school.

Generally, teachers start the morning by listing available activities. A child might spend the day on his first choice or he might not. Although there is a commitment to letting the children choose freely, in practice many teachers give work when they think it's needed. But to a very great extent the children really have a choice and go purposefully about their own work.

The classrooms are fairly noisy because the children can move and talk freely, and sometimes the teacher has to ask for quiet. However, when children work independently, discipline becomes less a problem than it is in a more formal classroom. When the class is taught as a unit, and every child is supposed to pay attention as the teacher talks, discipline can be a very serious matter. Quick children get restless; slow children are bored. In an open classroom, most children are usually absorbed, and those who are restless may go outdoors or play in the hallways.

The way children learn to read is an example of the kind of individual learning and teaching that goes on in an open classroom. At first it's hard to see just how children do learn, since there are no separate subjects. But after a while it becomes clear that, to a great extent, the children learn to read from each other. They hang around the library corners long before they can read, handling the books, looking at pictures, trying to find words they know, listening and watching as the teacher listens to other children reading.

There is an attempt to break down the mental barriers between the spoken, written, and printed word. Each child is given his own notebook for free writing. He may draw a picture in it, discuss the picture with the teacher, and dictate a caption to her which she writes down for him. He copies it just underneath. In this way he learns to memorize the look and sound of his dictated words and phrases until he reaches a point where, with help, he can write sentences.

In much the same way, children make their own dictionaries. Gradually the child amasses a reading and writing vocabulary and becomes fluent; you can see six-year-olds writing stories, free-verse poems, accounts of things done in class, all for an audience that includes other children as well as the teacher.

As a rule, teachers don't pay much attention to accuracy or neatness until a child is well along in his writing. Grammar, spelling, and punctuation are introduced after a time, not as separate subjects or ends in themselves, but as living ways to get meaning across.

The way math is taught further illustrates how classroom practice fuses with the ideas on child development that have shaped these new schools. Among the most important of these ideas is that primary school children learn basic mathematical concepts much more slowly than adults realize, and patterns of abstract thought used in mathematics must be built up from layer after layer of direct experience—seeing, hearing, feeling, smelling. A child learns how to sort and classify things—all sorts of everyday things—into sets, comparing the sizes of sets, the number of objects in each one. He learns how to count and to measure. He learns simple fractions, and aspects of addition, multiplication, and division as these arise from real situations in the classroom. He learns about shape and size and proportion by handling all sorts of concrete materials. What is important is not how much the children learn, but how much they understand. Rote learning and memorizing have been abandoned, partly because they bore children and teachers, but basically because they are poor ways to learn. Children are given an opportunity to watch children and talk to them about what puzzles or intrigues them. In this way, open schools are producing classes where mathematics is a pleasure and where, each year, there are fewer and fewer mathematical illiterates.

A word more ought to be said about the role of the teacher in an open structure school. Formal classroom teaching—the instructor standing up front talking to a group—has disappeared because it imposes a single pattern of learning on a whole group of children, and because it ignores the extent to which children teach each other. But even though the British infant schools stress cooperation and the children are encouraged to teach each other, there is no abdication of adult authority and no belief that this would be desirable. The role of the teacher remains crucial. A Leicestershire classroom in which the teacher is merely managing the room well enough, but not responding to individual children, is a very different place from one in which the teacher knows when to intervene, change the pace, ask a question or make a suggestion for the greatest learning advantage. These schools accept the real and legitimate authority of a teacher as an adult responsible for providing the kinds of experiences that will help children grow.

Most teachers working with children in an open structure setting are generally not preoccupied with the issue of freedom versus structure. The idea of giving children choices is a considered judgment about how they best learn. Freeing children is part of the point; encouraging them to make significant choices is desirable because often the choices reflect their needs, and in any case, this is how they learn to develop initiative, think for themselves and learn basic skills most effectively. But freedom by itself is seen as an empty educational aim. These schools are intent on teaching children to think. It is this deep pedagogical seriousness, the attention paid to learning in the classroom, which makes these schools different from many others that are superficially similar.

There are some problems associated with the open classroom. It is important that parents recognize and consider them before opting for this model.

- Most teachers are not trained to teach this way and the time needed for them to change, to adjust, will vary considerably. This means there will probably be a period of disorientation and disorganization on the part of both adults and children.

- The classrooms are not like those most parents are familiar with. They seem chaotic. They are noisy. It's often difficult for an observer to tell what's going on. Unless parents and administrators are willing to ask what is happening in the classroom and how a particular experience is important and at the same time help the teacher feel at ease, the open education approach will not work well.

- Teachers have historically not had to explain what they were doing or why. Again, the open approach will not work well unless they recognize that they must constantly question what they are doing *and* always be prepared to justify it to parents, administrators, *and* children.

- The classrooms often look messy—because so much is going on in so many places. In environments where streets and alleys are always filled with junk, this may turn off many parents. Staff must be quite sensitive to parents' feelings and prepared to work out a satisfactory approach with them.

- Improvement on standardized tests is often slower, although results even out over a period of years. It is nevertheless often difficult for parents to wait that long to see "progress."

An excellent description of how one teacher adopted this method in her classroom is found in the pamphlet, "An Interview with Pat Hourihan," published by the Education Development Center (see Chapter Twelve).

Montessori

In Rome, at the turn of the century, a young physician named Maria Montessori became interested in the education of young children, and in the course of her career developed a method of teaching which has had a profound effect on modern ideas about education generally and still serves as the basis for Montessori schools in Europe, Latin America, and the United States.

Dr. Montessori began to develop her methods while working with mentally retarded children, teaching them to take care of themselves, to be graceful and coordinated in movement, and eventually to read and write. Her graduates then entered regular schools and achieved as well as "normal" children. Her success with retarded children prompted her to try her methods with the working-class children who overran the poor districts of Rome and Milan largely unattended and unschooled, since their parents had to work and the government provided no schools or day care facilities. Her success in transforming these children into independent, purposeful youngsters who could read, write, and do numbers by the age of seven and were eager and joyful in their learning was a matter of tremendous interest to educators throughout the world. After a decline of interest for many years, her influence is once again widely felt, especially as the general public has come to believe in the importance of preschool education.

The Montessori method is a way of teaching that begins with very careful observations of what children of various ages are ready and eager to do. It assumes that children have a spontaneous interest in learning, in encountering their environment, in accepting challenges. Children are presented with a great variety of educational materials especially designed for each particular stage of mental and physical development, and they use these materials in sequence to teach themselves the various skills they want and need to learn at each stage. The role of the teacher is supportive. She may suggest an exercise to a child, offer help when a child requests it, or step in when a child becomes frustrated and can't figure a way out by himself, but the basic focus is on the child teaching himself and children teaching each other (hence the usual practice of having children of different ages in the same classroom).

The method is based on the belief that children can take responsibility for their own education, each proceeding at his own pace and in his own unique manner. The role of the adult is to provide a *prepared environment* that gives the child the means and assistance to educate himself and sets necessary limits so the child is not overwhelmed by too many choices or too much stimulation or left the prisoner of his impulses. Other fundamental beliefs are: all of a child's senses are interconnected and learning takes place through all of them; learning should be orderly and sequential; and children learn abstract ideas through experience with tangible, concrete things.

The first characteristic of a Montessori classroom environment is a warm, colorful, spacious room, immediately attractive to children and adults alike. Everything about it is child-sized: furniture, shelves and cabinets, washing and cleaning-up facilities, coathooks. There are plants and often animals and, wherever possible, an outdoor garden and play area. It is also orderly. There is a place for everything and one of the ground rules is that children return a game or toy to its place and clean up any mess before going on to another activity. However, as with most skills, this is taught by example of the teacher and older students rather than as a rigid rule by itself.

Children generally work either alone or in small groups at tables or on rugs. The children are free to move around, but encouraged to do so deliberately, with a purpose. In fact, they are encouraged to make deliberate choices about everything they do during the school day. A child may work with one set of learning materials as long as he wants and may return to it as often as he wants.

Maria Montessori developed materials in four basic areas for the 3- to 7-year-old child. These materials or modifications of them are still the basic ones for a Montessori classroom. The first is *practical life exercises,* through which children learn how to take care of their environment, take care of themselves, and be courteous to each other. Equipment here includes a child-sized but real kitchen and dining area where children can prepare, serve, and eat simple dishes. It also includes real brooms, mops, sponges, and other cleaning materials for the kitchen and classroom; gardening tools; irons and clothing to iron; practice boards to learn how to fasten buttons and snaps, tie shoelaces, tie bows, and manipulate zippers.

The second area is *sensorial materials,* to help the child develop each of his senses as finely as he can. It includes materials for developing discrimination of dimension, color, and form; of weight and sorting. Developing the senses keenly, and the coordination of the fine muscles of the hand, is regarded essential preparation for learning writing, reading, and mathematics later. An example of these materials are sets of ten cubes decreasing gradually in size from ten centimeters on a side to one centimeter on a side. The child learns to stack these on top of each other in the proper order by experimentation. There are often sets of ten items, increasing or decreasing in size or some dimension. This is in order to gradually prepare the children for arithmetic, and understanding our number system based on ten. Another characteristic of all Montessori materials is what's called the *isolation of difficulty*. Each item in a set of materials differs from another in only one respect, so as to teach the child that particular quality without confusing him. In other words, if the purpose is to teach the concept of thickness, all the items will be the same length, width, and color but each one in the series will be somewhat thicker than the other.

The final two areas are the actual materials for teaching mathematics and language, after the sensorial materials have laid the groundwork. Math materials include number rods, beads, counting boxes, sandpaper numerals. Language materials include sandpaper letters, word and picture cards, labels and labelling games, and various books and word games.

One of the more striking facts about Montessori schools is that children who attend them learn to read, write, and do arithmetic much sooner than children in conventional schools. In general, children in Montessori schools are writing by the time they are four and some learn when they are three-and-a-half. Children read somewhat later, but usually by the time they are five and most can do addition, subtraction, multiplication, and division of even very large numbers by the time they are six. The exercises by which children learn arithmetic exemplify the Montessori method: they are highly structured and sequential; they move from concrete objects to symbols and abstract ideas; they focus on the individual child working alone although some depend on the cooperation of several children; and they are designed so the child can measure his own progress and perfect his work.

The preparation for arithmetic begins with the sensorial materials. All blocks, cylinders, and many other toys are in sets of ten, increasing in size from one centimeter to ten centimeters in some dimension. So the child is gradually prepared for the first math exercise, which is teaching the numbers and symbols one to ten. The first exercise is a set of number rods, increasing in length from one centimeter to ten centimeters. As with all materials, the child takes up this exercise when he is ready, indicated by when he asks the teacher to show it to him or when the teacher asks him if he would like to do it and he responds positively. The teacher then takes the number rods over to a table or rug where the child wants to work. She demonstrates one way to do the exercise, for instance by naming each rod ("this is one") and then placing the rods on top of each other so as to form a staircase. Then she may conduct what Montessori calls the "three-period lesson." First she goes through each item, or maybe a few at a time, and names it: "this is one," "this is two," etc. Then she asks the child to point each one out as she says: "show me one," "show me two," etc. Finally, she puts them in front of the child one at a time, asking "what is this?" If a child makes a mistake in naming an item, the teacher does not correct him by saying "no" or "you're wrong," but instead backs up and repeats the lesson until the child grasps it. Then the teacher puts away the material (unless the child wants to use it by himself) and the child takes it out by himself whenever and as often as he wants to after that. The teacher never intervenes unless the child seems really frustrated or upset. The children are encouraged to use it however they want to, since the material itself is self-correcting. (For example, the staircase made out of number rods will look out of line if the child has placed some rods in the wrong order.) Once a child has mastered the material, he usually plays with it in all sorts of ways, making up his own unique games or getting other children to join him.

At the same time, the children are exposed to the sandpaper numerals, a series of hardboard cards with one numeral cut from sandpaper pasted to each one. The children learn the names of the numerals while tracing the sandpaper and feeling their shapes (so that they are learning to write the numerals at the same time). As soon as they have mastered both the number rods (concrete) and the sandpaper numerals (symbols, or abstract) they put the two together, matching up each rod with the corresponding numeral.

Then the child takes up the spindle box, which has a compartment for each number from zero to nine (this is the first time that the number zero is introduced) and a bunch of spindles. The set has the exact number of spindles required to count out the right number for each compartment.

Teachers often make up games for groups of children to play together which reinforce the concepts taught by the basic materials.

Next the children start learning the decimal system with materials known as the "Golden Beads." There are single beads, strings of ten beads, squares of one hundred beads, and cubes of one thousand beads. There are several exercises using the beads, so that children soon learn place value in numbers. There is one game called "The Crisis of Nine" in which the children learn that one more bead or number added to nine makes ten, which requires moving over to the next column or place. The children seem excited by the fact that they deal with large numbers, in the thousands, almost immediately. Once again, as soon as they have mastered the concrete numbers with the beads, they learn to match them up with the abstract symbols through number boards and overlapping cards.

Then they start adding, first with the beads again but translating each answer into numerals. They learn addition in a group at first, with each child responsible for picking out the right combination of beads for his number, placing it in a column with other children's numbers, and then all of them together counting up the total and selecting another set of beads to represent that. They learn subtraction in the same manner.

The game of skip counting lays the groundwork for multiplication. They lay out chains of beads made up of links of a given number of beads. For instance, they might start by counting by fives, connecting links of five beads each and tagging them at intervals indicating the cumulative total. Soon, they have learned the multiplication tables in this manner, having a great time stringing together long chains of beads numbering in the thousands and stretching all across the classroom. Once they have mastered multiplication and division concretely, they switch again to the abstract level and use big multiplication boards with movable numerals and then learn to use the abacus. They have long since begun writing the numerals themselves and therefore can transfer problems back and forth between the apparatus and their own paper.

Basic arithmetic skills have been mastered by children by the time they are six or seven. This leads to an important point to remember in considering the Montessori model as a possible curriculum baseline for your school: Maria Montessori's original work was done with three-to-seven-year-olds and even today the materials and methods of the Montessori school are most distinctive at that age level. Although Montessori herself later worked with older children and many modern Montessori schools go up through elementary school, classrooms for older children are less unique and often resemble, for instance, an open classroom of the Leicestershire or British infant school model. Furthermore, the basic Montessori method encompasses just the four areas mentioned above (practical life, sensorial development, language, and mathematics) and doesn't include music, science, social studies, or art. However, using the principles of the Montessori method like the isolation of difficulty, the three-period lesson, and moving from the concrete to the abstract and the known to the unknown, most Montessori teachers and schools have developed curricula in these areas as well.

A big problem for many considering starting a Montessori school is the cost of acquiring the basic materials and equipment. No firm in the United States manufactures them. They must be imported and are fairly expensive. However, much of the equipment can be made by parents and teachers themselves if they have the time and patience. And some U.S. manufacturers (such as Creative Playthings) make items very similar to certain of the Montessori materials. The best bet in considering this problem would be to find and consult a nearby, friendly Montessori school that is innovative in spirit and not determined to do everything exactly as it was done in the original Montessori schools.

That brings up another problem with Montessori education that has turned many Americans off: the tendency of official descendents of Maria Montessori's schools and training programs to develop a kind of religious orthodoxy and jealously guard all details of the original method. They seem to say that if you don't do it exactly the way Montessori herself did it, you're not truly following the Montessori method and cannot be recognized as a Montessori school. But this tends to preserve the letter rather than the spirit of Montessori's work. She regarded herself as a scientist and experimenter. The heart of her method was careful observation of young children and responding to what the children needed and wanted. She was constantly inventing new materials, equipment, and exercises as she gained new insights and perceptions of particular children. A true practitioner of her method would continually be experimenting and changing in tune with emerging perceptions of the particular children in a school and the particular community in which they reside.

Some critics have charged that the Montessori method's emphasis on children working with materials by themselves tends to neglect the children's emotional development and their ability to interact creatively and sensitively with other children. It is certainly true that Montessori herself was primarily interested in the development of the child's intellect, grace, and independence. However, creative Montessori teachers incorporate all sorts of opportunities for enhancing emotional growth and group interaction, for example, in discussions about stories the teacher reads to children or they write or read themselves and in outdoor classrooms and playgrounds. The emphasis, however, is on paying attention to the children's natural and spontaneous interest in these activities and discussions, rather than planning them in a particular way and according to a particular schedule. At one hour a Montessori classroom may be noisy and bustling with activity, at another time quiet as a library with everyone working on his own. Both are considered natural and valuable atmospheres.

The basic Montessori methods and materials are fairly easy to teach. Training programs for teachers last as a rule only one year. Much harder to teach is the central underlying skill of careful observation of children and the accompanying ability to respond to the endless varieties of their almost universal plea: "help me to do it myself." Montessori herself knew no way to teach this except practice and experience in working with children. As J. McV. Hunt said in his helpful introduction to the 1964 edition of *The Montessori Method:*

> If a teacher can discern what a child is trying to do in his . . . interaction with the environment, and if that teacher can have on hand materials relevant to that intention, if he can impose a relevant challenge with which the child can cope, supply a relevant model for imitation, or pose a relevant question that the child can answer, the teacher can call forth the kind of . . . change that constitutes psychological development or growth. This sort of thing was apparently the genius of Maria Montessori.

Caleb Gattegno: Educational Solutions, Inc.

Caleb Gattegno is becoming widely known as the inventor-developer of some increasingly popular educational materials, especially the Cuisinaire Rods for teaching mathematics and the Words in Color reading program. It is unfortunately not widely known that he and his colleagues have developed a clear, comprehensive approach to education, with practical applications to most of the basic curricular areas.

The basic business of traditional education is the transmission of knowledge (produced by gifted people over the ages) by teachers, and the acquisition of this knowledge by students through the power of memory. The trouble with this view, according to Gattegno, is that memory is one of the weaker powers of the mind. Schools seem to tacitly acknowledge this by providing all sorts of props for students—presentation, classroom exercises, homework, review, tests, more exercises, more homework, more review, more tests, and so on, year after year. Furthermore, schools expect that children don't know very much when they begin their schooling, especially so-called disadvantaged or culturally deprived children.

Gattegno is instead quite impressed with the tremendous powers of mind and interest in learning all children have before they even start school. They have taught themselves thousands of things already, often working hour after hour, day after day, to learn a new skill, such as sitting up or walking. In particular, they have learned a language, probably the most difficult learning task anyone ever undertakes—and this usually by the time the child is two years old! Gattegno is quite impressed with the powers of mind demonstrated by children in such learning, and he spent many years studying these powers in detail. His methods of education are built on making use of and developing the powers of mind children already have when they come to school.

For example, he points out that reading and writing are simply somewhat different forms of the language children already know how to speak. He believes teachers need only teach children the code used in written language to represent spoken language, and then point out that otherwise it's the same thing they already know (rather than some strange, large new body of "knowledge"). Furthermore, children can learn this code quickly from materials that are basically games. He believes and has demonstrated that anyone can learn to read in two or three months.

Similarly, he believes the basic principles of algebra and logic (such as understanding abstraction, transformation of meaning from one situation to another, substitution of symbols) are already possessed by young children, again having been learned in the process of learning language. So he would have teachers open the world of mathematics to children on the basis of these powers of mind they already have, rather than by rote processes. One teacher who used these methods in teaching math to second graders found that "my second graders, who knew very little math when we began, explored addition, subtraction, multiplication, division, powers and roots, and different bases, with depth of understanding far beyond my previous classes. I could see that my students were beginning to free their minds from reliance on rote processes. They were beginning to use their minds to think creatively in mathematics and derive their own original ways to solve problems. They were beginning to see that the answer was not so important as the thinking that went into it. . . . With no apologies or attempts to make the material 'relevant' we moved the children into some quite abstract processes; and they loved it. They loved it because the thinking was fun; and because what they learned and the thinking they did made them feel so smart and powerful."

Gattegno's approach has been extended into the teaching of foreign languages, social studies, science, literature, art, music, and physical education. There are several books by Gattegno and his colleagues describing the approach and the specific curricula in various areas. The best way to learn about it in detail, however, is through the inexpensive workshops held in various parts of the country by the organization of which Gattegno is director, Educational Solutions, Inc. (See Chapter Twelve for more details).

Making Your Own Curriculum

You may choose to select one of these models as the basic organizing focus for your curriculum or you may select aspects from several models and merge them according to your own needs. If you wish to base your school on a particular model already in existence, explore the method carefully to be sure your goals and the results of that method are compatible. Remember any method can be changed and adapted to your situation. And remember to test your method and use your own judgment about whether it works. Don't be afraid to change your methods as you go along. Lots of experimenting is in order.

The following are some examples of schools which have made their own curriculum from scratch or adapted a model to the particular circumstances of their students or community.

East Harlem Block Schools

There will be forces operating within each school and community which will influence the content and structure of the curriculum. One of the most basic of these influences is the needs of your particular neighborhood, its unique people and problems and styles.

The East Harlem Day School, the elementary school unit of the parent-controlled East Harlem Block Schools, has about 110 children from one of the poorest neighborhoods in New York City. Most of the children are Puerto Rican, though a substantial minority are black and a few are white. It has grown out of the nursery school, one grade at a time, and now has five grades.

Each classroom has a teaching team comprised of a professional teacher and an assistant teacher who is a parent. Most of the administrative staff, including the executive director, are also parents. The continually evolving curriculum is created largely by the professional teachers, but under the guidance and ultimate control of the parents. The parents want the curriculum to give the children the personal power necessary to survive in a racist society and a faith in their collective power to change or replace the institutions which affect their lives.

During the first year, the curriculum and structure were that of a free school. The parents later rejected this model because the children were not making sufficient progress in learning the basic skills of reading and arithmetic. The parents felt then and continue to feel now that basic academic skills are the first requirement of a curriculum for every child.

During the second year the teachers concentrated on developing a strong reading and mathematics curriculum that continues to be basic to the school. In mathematics, they use the approach of Caleb Gattegno and Madeleine Goutard based on the Cuisenaire Rods and the assumption that children can learn a lot of abstract math very quickly. The children liked this approach because it was fun and because it made each of them feel intelligent. They liked to think mathematically and abstractly. The teachers made no attempt initially to relate mathematics to practical problems and applications. The children do this later on their own.

The reading curriculum is more eclectic. The first-grade teacher starts with the organic approach of Sylvia Ashton-Warner. Children learn to sight-read and then to write words that are powerful for them personally. They trade words with each other. After a few months, once they have perceived the basic notion that reading is merely another form of the spoken language they already know, the teachers start phonics and other decoding skills. Teachers use phonics materials from several sources, including Gattegno's Words in Color program and the Sullivan Reading Materials.

The parents and staff also consider it important that children begin to learn about science and scientific thinking. The heart of the Day School's science curriculum is the series of units and materials developed by the Educational Development Center (EDC) known as the Elementary Science Series. Most of these are presented as experiments in which children record their observations in a notebook and build and compare their discoveries. Individual teachers have developed units on the human body, animal behavior, and various kinds of nature study. Older children go together on a ten-day trip to a farm each spring during which they do intensive study of natural science.

Social studies is the current focus of the curriculum-building process. The content has come from things on the kids' minds and from parents' concern for developing cultural pride and solidarity. One of the most successful units dealt with the use of drugs in the community. The kids see junkies every day and are both fascinated by and afraid of drugs. The unit combined the personal experiences of parents and several ex-addicts with scientific and medical facts compiled by the professional teacher. Another successful series was one dealing with sex education. This year, the fourth-grade class is doing an extensive study of Puerto Rican history.

In classroom organization and the structure of the day, the Day School has been influenced strongly by the open classroom or British infant school model. However, each teaching team is free to structure its classroom as it wishes, so long as the students are learning the basic skills and are happy and engaged during the day. Teachers often modify the degree of structure several times during the school year.

Some classes alternate throughout the day between periods of structured lessons or group activity (usually in small groups) and periods of free exploration and interaction with the various materials around the classroom. Other teachers concentrate the structured activity in the morning and leave the afternoon free for individual activity or field trips. Still another teacher may follow the open format for the entire day, but will work in a carefully planned way to draw individual children or groups of children into different kinds of work challenging to them. Even during an entirely open day, each child will typically have several assignments, such as a requirement to write a page or two in his notebook.

Nearly every class has two or three discussions each day involving the entire group. This is a way for teachers and children to share responsibility for the classroom and for planning in particular. It is also a time for discussing interpersonal problems in the classroom, on the playground, on the street, or at home. These discussions also contribute a great deal to forging a genuine unity in the class.

A common principle in all classrooms is to have frequent discussions of students' work on an individual basis in subjects such as art or math. A key purpose of such discussions is to highlight the discoveries of individual children and make them available to the whole group.

Each class also has a quiet period every day, lasting from twenty to forty-five minutes depending on age. The only rule is that no one can talk to anyone else. Most children read or write or do some other quiet activity. Parents and teachers consider this especially important to these children whose lives at school and home are otherwise quite crowded and noisy.

The Learning Place

The Learning Place, a junior-senior high school in San Francisco, is an example of a school for older children which has adapted some of the open structure and Summerhillian ideas used by others for younger children. The Learning Place, though, has recognized the limitations of that philosophy in an urban setting. Children do need lots of freedom to be themselves and move at their own pace in learning. But they also must learn how to deal with this freedom in a constructive manner, and with the complicated and often hostile environment of our cities. A "free" school in a large city is very different from a boarding school in the country.

The students at The Learning Place come from lower and middle class homes. There is diversity, including some students with emotional problems, some with strong aversion to academic pursuits, some who are extremely bright, others who are angry and have many problems relating to their parents.

The curriculum is hard to capture because it's constantly evolving and changing to meet the needs of the students and the school community. One month may see a heavily scheduled academic course, the next month will be camping trips and working on building their space. The types of activities are greatly varied. There may be a classroom situation with a teacher and students pursuing a specific discipline: math, spelling, biology. Or the students may be having direct experiences in the community: setting up a breakfast program for elementary children, visiting a court session, planning and executing a trip to Grand Canyon, working out school-community problems. Or the students may become involved with teachers or other adults on a personal, tutorial basis, learning through apprenticeships, conversations, intellectual explorations, activities.

The primary principle is that the learning needs and patterns of each student are different. There should be a variety of settings and opportunities to meet these needs and patterns. Another principle is that the child will learn a wide range of skills and facts when he is not afraid of failure and when his natural desire to know has not been crushed. The staff believe that as long as the child is told what to learn under very rigid conditions, with rote learning being the primary method, he will never explore for himself what he can do best; he will be a slave to what others say he should do and think and learn.

At this point in the development of the curriculum at The Learning Place, students and staff are beginning to ask for more discipline and depth in academic areas. After two years of lots of playing and some good work, they are moving toward seriously pursuing interests in art, carpentry, sciences, general skills of reading, writing, spelling, and math, and, most important, emotional and social development.

The students' request for disciplined academic work comes from real excitement about learning. No one is forcing them to spend hours understanding genetics or algebra—they *want* to learn and the teachers enjoy teaching them. As a result, the time required to learn a course is drastically reduced. Moreover, while it might be that a "required" curriculum would not differ from what students study at The Learning Place, the difference in motivation between "required" and desired is critical.

Highland Park Free School

Highland Park Free School is a parent-controlled school with about 200 students drawn from the predominantly poor Black community of Highland Park in Boston. Each classroom is run by a community teacher with the assistance of a professional teacher. The ages of students are equivalent to kindergarten through eighth grade.

Since the start of the school there has been tension between educational experimentation and the feelings of some parents that learning basic skills requires a highly structured classroom like that of the public schools the parents remember. In spite of this tension there are substantial differences among the many classrooms in the school, since each teacher team is in charge of its own class. Increasingly, however, the school has been moving toward sharing certain parts of the curriculum throughout the school. This effort is a result of an increasing awareness by parents and teachers of the mutual needs of the students, the Highland Park community, and the Black community generally.

The classrooms are less rigidly structured than most public schools, but more structured than the British infant school or Montessori classrooms. A typical day for six- and seven-year-olds would include:

> Breakfast: this period stresses responsibilities for the students in serving, cleaning, setting up the classroom, feeding animals, etc. The purpose is to teach that the class belongs to the students in the sense that it cannot function without their help.

Yoruba Songs and Recitation of *Ngozo Saba*: the seven principles, followed by small group discussion of one of these guiding principles or of some issue brought up by students or teachers.

Reading hour: the class will typically be divided into four groups of 5 or 6 students, each working on a separate project. One group may be using phonics flash cards, one practicing letter formation, one reading out loud, and one writing stories about pictures. Teachers move from group to group providing help and encouragement where needed.

Mathematics: another hour devoted to number skills and organized in the same small group fashion with students working at their own pace.

Science or social studies project: this may be, for example, drawing a map of the neighborhood or of a country being studied.

In each of these morning sessions there are specific tasks students are encouraged to complete. Recesses are spread throughout.

Lunch

Afternoon: This time is generally less structured and resembles models like the British infant school. There are many materials available and students pick any project they want to work on. Student interest is the center of the curriculum at this point, although this interest is sometimes organized into trips or projects done by the entire class (an urban studies project once made a map of how different land was used in the neighborhood). Some activities are outside the school, such as dance, music, and art work offered at the Elma Lewis Center in Roxbury.

The vehicle for providing some curriculum common to all the classes has been the *Ngozo Saba,* seven principles adapted from Nyrere's principles of African Socialism. These were first introduced after the director returned from a visit to Africa during which he became convinced of the importance of rituals which could provide an implicit, symbolic organization for the school and replace the irrelevant rituals of public schools (e.g., flag salute). The principles are: unity;

self-determination; collective work and responsibility; cooperative economics; purpose; creativity; and faith. These were adopted by the parents and staff readily as an expression of values important to their community. In addition to using them in morning ritual and discussion, the school attempts to relate these principles to most discussions in the classroom (e.g., what did we do today to make ourselves more unified as a class or how does this historical movement reflect antagonism to cooperative economics?), and to discussion in teacher's meetings of classroom situations. As time goes on the meaning of these principles to the community has become obvious in concrete situations, and the principles have thereby become the beginning of a curriculum common to all the classes in the school.

The *Ngozo Saba* describe some of the values the school feels are needed in order to help develop strong individuals with self-respect and a commitment to the Black community. The structured situation in the class, especially mornings, reflects the need to provide unity between home and school. It has been found by the school that too much tension between the often highly structured home and a wide-open classroom makes it difficult for students to function well. It's not a matter of discipline, but of creating enough structure for a child to feel comfortable and confident about making his or her own decisions.

There has also been an increase in the school's analysis of the technical skills the community will need in the future. Skills are stressed which students do not bring to school with them. For example, standard English is taught, but almost as if it were a second language. The message is that street language is adequate and important, but that standard English must also be learned in order to get along in the technocratic white culture. It is like learning to speak French when going to France. No putdown of the mother tongue is implied, only a recognition of a skill needed to get along in another world.

Math and science are also stressed since it has become increasingly apparent to the school that there are not enough people with technical skills in the Black community. The school feels that if students can get excited about math and science at a young age, it will lead them naturally into technical expertise later.

Throughout the school there is an attempt to select or make materials relevant to the urban, Black experience, and related to the *Ngozo Saba.* The community is often a resource, providing useful materials and a reason to be concerned with what is being learned.

Staff and parent curriculum committees have increasingly focused on getting teachers and parents to reflect on community goals so that curriculum and materials can be made with the needs of the community in mind.

The Group School

The Group School is a student- and staff-run high school for working-class youth in Cambridge, Massachusetts. Its curriculum and entire program are a response to the needs of working-class youth and the social and economic pressures of a working-class neighborhood. The Group School accepts the ideas of its students about what education is—learning from experience—and tries to help every student become a self-motivated learner.

The curriculum is constantly evolving, but its core includes basic skills, employment, working-class history and culture, and personal growth. The basic skills program responds to the need of these 14-to-21-year-olds to sharpen those skills not adequately developed in public schools. No student is required to take basic skills, but most do in fact involve themselves in one of the many different reading and math programs available. There are courses in remedial reading and math as well as in higher levels of these skills needed for college entrance examinations, high school equivalency examinations, or creative writing.

The employment program aims to meet the needs of these students to have gainful employment to support themselves and their families, and to eliminate the need for any student to choose between work and study in order to preserve his or her self-esteem. The program places students in jobs and provides personal counseling and seminars dealing with the problems of work, the structure of working situations, and future work plans. The Group School is also developing plans for vocational counseling and eventually vocational training.

Working-class history and culture, embodied in the entire attitude of the school but focused on in a course called "Hard Times," provides an opportunity for students to understand the labor history of which their parents and grandparents were a part and to relate these experiences to a political and economic analysis of the present world of work. It is a history of America viewed through the eyes of the working class. Here, as elsewhere in the school, much teaching is done through role playing, projects, and examination of the real issues facing the students. A women's history class focuses on contributions and problems of women in a male-dominated society.

The Group School also pays considerable attention to the emotional growth and needs of students, especially because this concern has been passed over or repressed by the public schools from which they came. There are encounter groups, including one women's group, and considerable personal counseling aimed at helping everyone recognize and express his or her own feelings. To some the school has taken on the aspect of a family—open and not so judgmental as to discourage personal expression.

The school also provides opportunities for students to pursue whatever their personal goals may involve. There are craft workshops; music, drama, science, law, and politics classes; and sports. And the school has a large group of volunteer teachers who provide instruction in any subject students show an interest in.

Personal services, often through referrals to cooperating agencies, are also a basic part of the school's effort to provide all the assistance students need in getting a sound education. Physical and mental health, legal, employment, and family problems are among those the school helps students deal with. Any problem preventing a student from gaining full value from his education is treated as a personal concern by the school and no issue involving a member of the school community is considered irrelevant or beyond the scope of the school's purpose.

CHAPTER EIGHT

Curriculum: Important Questions

In this chapter we will discuss several problems commonly faced by people building a curriculum for a new school.

Basic Skills

Controversies have often centered on the manner in which basic academic skills are taught and the general emphasis such teaching is given. You can eliminate much of this potential conflict by thinking carefully and clearly about basic skills as you build your curriculum.

What fundamental skills are necessary, in your view, for later learning and ultimately for survival in the world? Few groups would disagree that reading, writing, and basic arithmetic are essential skills. Most communities will add others to the list of basic skills, such as fluency in two languages. How soon must basic skills be learned? How are you going to teach these basic skills? Or how are you going to provide for children to learn them on their own?

Sometimes, people starting new schools, especially if they aren't parents themselves and aren't in close touch with parents, slide over these questions quickly. They might say, for example, "Learning skills is not as important as being in a loving, healthy environment where the child can develop freely. Anyway, in a rich and caring environment, children will want to learn most skills on their own." That may be a valid approach, but unless it is very well thought out and accepted by everyone in the school, there will be a lot of anxiety and maybe even hard feelings later when some children are *not* in fact learning to read and write. You must be sure that your judgment about the importance of basic skills reflects the needs of the students and not a fanciful idea of the kind of world they are going to have to cope with.

On the other hand, in some schools parents' valid concerns about learning basic skills have led to very rigid priorities for teaching them. In the worst settings, like many public schools, teaching skills is regarded as the only important thing and everything else is considered a "frill." But even in new schools, where parents and teachers understand that children learn most and best in an environment where they're happy and respected, parent (and teacher) anxiety may create a lot of pressure on the teachers and children and may force adoption of a rigid timetable. This can be as harmful as ignoring basic skills.

Look at the experience of other schools which have experimented with different approaches to teaching skills, in more free and open contexts. Results have generally been good when parents trusted teachers who were serious about teaching and really cared about the kids, even though parents were initially skeptical of their methods. Some new schools have been pleasantly surprised themselves at how well their graduates have done when they entered traditional public high schools.

Here are some guideposts:

- Think carefully about what skills you consider important.
- Think carefully about how you propose to teach them.
- Don't be afraid to try very different and unusual methods if they make sense to you.
- Make sure all your parents understand very thoroughly the school's approach to the learning of skills.
- Make sure the staff is regularly accountable to parents on children's progress.

Structure

Parents starting a school may be disturbed at the seeming lack of structure in some other new schools they visit or have heard about. When they don't see kids sitting in desks or all working quietly at tables (in other words, when they do not see the only classroom structure they have personally experienced), they are afraid kids can do anything they want, and consequently will not learn.

In fact, there are many different ways of structuring a classroom that don't much resemble a traditional school. It's important to go beyond the initial fears of chaos and no-learning and look beneath the surface for the structure. At first glance, for instance, an open classroom along the lines of the Leicestershire model may seem noisy and disorganized. Closer inspection would show, however, that the environment provides a lot of structure—there are a limited number of materials around and planned activities from which children choose. These materials are carefully selected and activities are carefully planned not only to allow children to express their own feelings and ideas and progress at their own rate, but also to insure that each activity of a child's day contributes to his learning and growing in areas parents and staff consider essential. Furthermore, the teacher is quietly moving among individual children and groups of children, helping those who are frustrated, suggesting new possibilities to some children, and mediating conflicts among children who would otherwise become destructive. He or she is a basic part of the structure. There are, in addition, certain rules about how children treat one another and how they care for materials. Even if these rules are few and simple, they provide another element of structuring the activity in the classroom.

Finally, the examples presented by the adults' behavior are a part of the structure. Very little about this seemingly chaotic situation has not been carefully planned and structured, and the results are often very impressive. Sometimes you will find adults in fact *have* tried to avoid creating and imposing structure, even one as open as in a Leicestershire classroom. They have usually done so because they believe any structure imposed by adults (other than that naturally flowing from their personalities) is artificial and limits the natural creativity and curiosity of children. However, in such cases, the vacuum does not last long. The kids themselves create a structure. They establish rules and patterns of behavior they enforce or attempt to enforce with each other. If you choose to let the students create their own structure, you should watch this evolving structure closely to see whether it's actually helping the kids learn and grow happily.

The students in elementary school haven't much experience in making social structures work. Even though they may be free of many of the hangups and bad habits of their elders, they are still young and some of them may have been hurt and distorted by unhealthy structures and insensitive treatment before. Therefore, sometimes the kids evolve structures that are not helpful to learning and yet don't change them because they don't know what is making them unhappy. If adults don't intervene, or wait too long to do so, these patterns may destroy the school and/or cause a lot of pain and unhappiness to the kids. Shire School in San Francisco, for example, functioned fairly well for a number of years with loving teachers who imposed very little structure. Then one fall and winter, for reasons which are not clear, the student body began to split into generally hostile and uncooperative factions. More and more the school was consumed by fighting, bickering, and stealing. For a while the staff stood back, expecting this to be a phase the kids had to pass through in learning to live and work together. As the situation became more and more painful, they tried to intervene, but by then the children were unresponsive to anything the staff thought of and finally the staff and some of the parents decided they had no choice but to close the school.

If the structure of your curriculum is designed to provide freedom for students to make choices for their own learning (and learn to take responsibility for their own learning by living with the results of those choices—learning from mistakes as well as successes), you need to look at it carefully from time to time to make sure it's actually doing that. Sometimes, having too many choices limits rather than broadens freedom—a student may easily become bewildered and confused and then either withdraw and do very little or become angry and interfere with the learning of others.

There are some schools which purport to offer unlimited choice, where each student is encouraged to decide what he wants to learn. Even here there are often hidden pressures, expectations, or structures which limit choice. It is better to have these things clear than to presume there are no bounds to the freedom in the school. Unlimited choice is aimed for. It may work very well among older students who are self-motivated already and have some clear notions of what they want to do. But for younger students, and others who have previously been almost totally dependent upon external authority for directing their education, a situation of unlimited choice may limit their freedom severely. Insurmountable confusion is not freedom.

Fortunately, these situations of too much choice or unclear restrictions on choice can be changed fairly easily if you are closely and frequently observing what's happening. You can limit the number of choices for a while, if students seem to be getting generally frustrated. On the other hand, you can open up the structure—creating more choices and encouraging individuals to develop their own activities— when there seems to be a lot of "champing at the bit" or boredom. You can examine what pressures students feel and see if these are the desired product of your structure or lack of it. As students grow older and more experienced in handling freedom creatively, you will want to modify your structure accordingly.

In summary, we want to emphasize that the question of structure need not be an emotionally charged issue in which the choice is between structure and no structure. There are plenty of different kinds of structure, if you will take the time to look for them. There is really no such thing as an unstructured school. The real question is whether your structure (whether you designed it or it just happened) is working for you; whether it is promoting the kind of learning and interaction and happiness among the kids that you want. If not, it can be adjusted from time to time with small and moderate changes, so long as you observe closely what's going on and don't allow destructive situations to persist.

Politics and Curriculum

A third question commonly discussed and sometimes avoided, concerns the political impact of the curriculum. If we think of politics as the power relationships between people or groups, then every school is both an expression of a political situation and a teacher of politics. Textbooks or teachers may totally avoid advocating political positions but the school will still have political implications, and it's best to admit this and examine your reactions to it.

Every school has a political structure. The general governing method represents the power of varying people—staff, parents, kids, other community members—over decisions made at the school. This will serve as a model from which students will draw certain conclusions about what should or should not be the relationships of these people and of people generally. If you discover differences between the values you hold and the values your school structure represents, you will no doubt want to make some change.

Just as with student selection and governance, there are choices in teaching methods which have political implications and effects. The relationship among teachers and the relationship between teachers and director or teachers and students expresses values about the relative allocation of power over different kinds of decisions. At the Iron-bound Community School considerable thought has been given to this problem in the context of a white working-class neighborhood with traditionally strong views about authority. The parents have decided after examining the development of their own childhood, that the teachers, assistant teachers, and parent volunteers should be in a rela-tion of absolute equality as regards power in the classroom, and their relationship to the kids. To do otherwise, they believe, would be to foster undesirable notions of hierarchy among people.

The same kinds of implications stem from the degree of coopera-tiveness or competition fostered among children—how much rules and regulations take the place of personal relationships, the effect of grad-ing, tracking, or other differentiating among students, etc. It is easy to believe in political neutrality, but the reality seems to be that basic values about power and human organization are taught by subtler examples than textbook instruction.

You may well find conflict in yourself between the ideals you hold and what you perceive as the most practical or efficient method of getting your school to do what you want it to do. We may teach the importance of democracy, but run our schools as an autocracy in order to get things done. We may ask children to get along with one another, but only regard them in competitive struggles. The political effects of your methods should not be ignored when it comes to figuring out whether you are reaching your goals. These effects are as real and perhaps as important as whether reading is learned.

What Process of Curriculum Decision Will You Use?

The experience of many new schools involves slow, trial-and-error development. This is especially true of curriculum, which, for the majority of schools, seems to be the last area to receive careful, well-organized attention. This is not entirely surprising, since the struggle for survival often takes much of the energy people would like to apply to the pursuit of excellence. The process of curriculum decision is fragmentary until people suddenly see it as a neglected area and treat it with special energy.

The chief exception to trial-and-error development is found in those schools adhering to a specific curriculum theory developed by people outside the school. The programmed, sequential use of materials characteristic of the Montessori method is a good example. Though minor modifications are often made, those who use the method find most of the decisions about what to teach and how to teach have already been made.

If your school grows out of some organizing principle other than a curriculum model, there will be much greater need for a process of planning curriculum with which you are comfortable. The parameters of this process may be set by decisions you have already made about your school. For example, a school which places a high degree of importance on parent participation will adopt a process by which parents can influence or control the basic aspects of curriculum.

In setting up a method of making curriculum decisions, provide for the following:

1. *Formulation of curriculum plans in advance.* This will involve a process of translating the general goals into a teaching plan (for example, that reading and math skills should be taught in both English and Spanish, but that no child should be pressured to learn English before age 9 if his natural inclination is to work with art materials or work in Spanish). This planning process must take adequate account of the interests of parents and teachers alike so that everyone will be able to support the decisions once they are made. Since few people are aware of the many different kinds of curricula, the group you set up to make these decisions may want to do some studying on its own, for example through a set of seminars, or through requesting staff to present a number of alternative plans. If you have a curriculum committee, there should be some way for it to relate its work back to the entire parent or community body.

2. *Reactions of teachers, students, parents.* When the curriculum is in operation, there will be reactions about its usefulness. You should pay attention to the teachers', parents', and students' evaluation. It may be that the curriculum is not comfortable

for teachers, is beyond their skills or is turning the kids off. Some system of discussing these reactions should be set up, for example, monthly discussions among teachers and parents on how a program is working out. Such evaluation should probably not be left until the end of the year, because many modifications can be made during the year. Being responsive is something a small school can do well. Remember it's just as important that teachers feel productive and parents feel supportive as that students learn, because all these are tied together. Testing may be part of this process, but it will not answer many important questions about emotional development.

3. *Making changes.* In some situations, the group monitoring reactions to the curriculum may not be the same as the group that set up the curriculum in the first place. The involvement of teachers and students may be heavier. In any case, it should not be a giant struggle for the monitoring group to get action on its perceptions. Don't set up a structure that separates planning and action so completely that you cannot move back and forth between them easily. This may amount to nothing more than maintaining some intimacy among all the people involved in curriculum decisions. *Don't bureaucratize.*

4. *Getting new information from outside.* Knowing about other schools' experiences is often the most neglected area of curriculum decisions. Undoubtedly, a number of schools have similar goals and students. They can probably be located through the New Schools Directory. There are also groups which make it their business to develop curriculum materials and ideas and help schools and parents get acquainted with different approaches. If you want to improve your curriculum, you should probably keep in touch with these groups and schools (see Chapter Twelve, *Resources*). Some way of introducing this kind of information should be built into your curriculum decision process, for it is easy to overlook.

Some schools have seminars for parents or for the curriculum committee(s) during the year. Others hold such sessions during planning time or during summer. Sometimes outside help is sought in response to a particular problem; for example, parents may be interested in textbooks, but really have little experience in evaluating them.

Whatever the process, it's a matter of maintaining education for teachers and parents as well as students. This is one of the big benefits of a small school with heavy involvement of all segments of its community. The education of parents and teachers about what is going on in the school and how it can be improved, the spreading of educational "expertise" throughout the community, is not just a luxury. Many schools which have inaugurated new teaching methods without the involvement of parents have experienced serious confrontations about how the school is run. It is an inevitable collision unless the process of curriculum decision involves parents and staff together and unless attention is paid to educating parents and staff as well as students.

The relative influence of students, teachers, directors, parents, experts, and the community at large varies tremendously from school to school:

- One school leaves curriculum planning totally up to the individual teacher in the individual classroom. The teacher may or may not involve other people in his decisions.

- Another school has four parent curriculum committees developing curriculum ideas for teachers to carry out in communications, social science, natural science, and math.

- Still another has a parent curriculum committee which doesn't plan, but listens to parent complaints and seeks adjustments to satisfy them. It also runs curriculum workshops for parents to increase parent planning of curriculum.

- The school director had considerable influence on curriculum matters but the school later moved to group decisions by the teaching staff because people felt more self-respect working this plan.

- One school has an elaborate curriculum decision process in which authority rests with parents, but the entire staff and the educational director are involved. There are daily meetings of teachers and assistant teachers to evaluate the day and plan the next day; weekly meetings with the teachers and education director to discuss curriculum problems and student and staff reactions; monthly meetings of the entire staff and parents, to talk about curriculum practice and philosophy; voluntary workshops by experts on new curriculum materials or methods; and two-week workshops in September on curriculum planning.

- Another school makes curriculum by hiring staff with particular interests.
- Another school's curriculum is based largely on the expressed interests of students working on projects.
- One school spent ten weeks in parent seminars discussing everything from the psychology of young children to their own experiences in school before deciding on the kind of curriculum they wanted. They then simply hired teachers who shared their philosophy and created personal relationships among parents and teachers sufficient to exchange reactions and change plans when needed.

Perhaps the most important factor in making a curriculum decision process satisfactory is that the school be small enough to allow direct participation of everyone who wants to be involved. A predominance of curriculum experts or curriculum administrators seems to be a reaction to a school so large that it's impractical for parents, teachers, and students to participate fully in these vital decisions.

CHAPTER NINE

Evaluation Questions

Student Growth and Progress. Will the school give grades to students? Will it otherwise comparatively rank them or their progress?

Will the school have testing? Diagnostic testing? Standardized testing similar to that of the public schools? Experimental, e.g., "culture-free," testing trying to measure ability and/or achievement in different ways? Tests within the classrooms or instructional program?

Should there be regular evaluative conferences between teachers and students? Teachers and parents? All three together? Will the teachers write regular written reports on the progress of children? How will students evaluate their own progress?

School Self-Evaluation. Does the school wish to adopt some regular, conscious procedures for evaluating its progress or success?

Do you want to specify goals such that later on you can concretely evaluate to what extent you have reached them?

How often do you want to evaluate? Weekly? Monthly? Annually? Different times for different aspects?

Do you want to evaluate in informal, but perhaps regular, meetings?

Do you want to engage a consultant or volunteer not directly associated with the school to advise you on evaluation, and perhaps to gather some data to feed back to parents, staff, students?

Outside Independent Evaluations. Do you wish to arrange for some sort of outside evaluation by an independent person or group? For what reasons? Under what conditions? How closely do you want to work with them?

If a community school, how about some sort of community evaluating team or process (analogous to teams of visiting professional educators that evaluate schools for the regional accrediting associations)?

What stance are you going to take toward outside agencies—state or local school district—or colleges that may approach you wanting to evaluate the school for purposes of their own?

Evaluation by Prospective Parents. How do you want prospective parents to evaluate your school? In other words how should a parent decide whether or not to send his/her child to your school?

Do you wish your self-evaluation to be oriented in this way? Do you want to have an outside evaluation designed for this purpose? Do you want testing and achievement scores and data available to prospective parents?

Have you considered making up a checklist of things a prospective parent should do in considering and evaluating your school?—talking to one or two other parents already in the school, visiting a classroom for at least half a day, talking with one or more teachers, looking over some of the instructional materials, carefully reading the school's statement of goals, comparing your school with at least one other school, stating clearly his or her expectations of your school so that you can discuss honestly with the parent whether or not you believe the school will meet those expectations and what problems might arise.

CHAPTER TEN

Fund Raising

It would be great if we could offer an optimistic report on the possibilities of raising money to support community schools. But the truth of the matter is that it is a long, hard road and many people spend more energy on fund raising than on education. Good hustling, hard work, and a little luck can keep your school afloat for a time, but eventually we all face the problem of finding some reliable, stable source of income. It is this goal which you should keep in mind and toward which your other funding strategies should build.

It is important to understand the political and economic context into which community schools are born. To receive public tax money a school must be part of a system which is administered by a locally elected school board. Unless you are setting up a community school within the public system through the exercise of your own political power or the benevolence of that system, you are beginning *outside* the definition of schools which will be supported by tax monies. You may get some of the crumbs from the tax table, but basically you will either have to depend on private support or struggle to change the way school money is distributed. Most of this section deals with getting private support or tax table crumbs, but these sources cannot sustain a community school for very long. Most community schools must sooner or later face the issue of getting public funds.

Those who elect to set up their own schools by taking over a piece of the public system, elect to confront the issue of getting resources first. Those who begin outside the system may be able to build a good school and they may be able to build internal strength and political support by deferring the confrontation, but sooner or later they will probably either face this problem or dissolve. We note with some anger that our economic system and the present method of funding education allows the rich to avoid the issue of getting public funds for the education of their choice while the poor and the working class must constantly struggle with that issue.

Tuition

Many schools examine the idea of having a tuition at some time in their history. Often this is not practical because parents simply cannot afford tuition. Other schools feel that tuition violates their beliefs even if some parents could afford to pay. And schools with tuition often supplement their income from other sources.

If you are considering imposing some kind of tuition, it is not difficult to construct a system of graduated tuitions based on the ability of each family to pay. Strict income-tuition figures are usually not useful because the decision of what a family can "afford" is so personal and so much a reflection of other expenses they may have. Setting up some general guidelines, such as a maximum tuition and an average tuition for broad categories of income, is best. These can be used as the basis of discussion between the school and the parents about what can be afforded. These negotiations should be private. Keeping tuition amounts confidential may help avoid embarrassment and pressure.

Private Aid

Private assistance may come from local individuals and businesses, from local foundations, or from national foundations. You want to develop your own funding strategy based on where you think you can be most effective; but a few schools have discovered some general rules of thumb about the private assistance route.

First, most national foundations will want to know whether you have attempted to raise money locally. Being able to enumerate local attempts, successful or not, may help you to be taken more seriously. Local individuals, especially ones whose positions or numbers might impress other people with money, can be very helpful. You are trying to break into a world in which a relatively small group of people respect the opinions of each other or people "like them." Once a few of these people give you money, you have begun to acquire the "respectability" which can be used to convince still more people of the merits of your request.

In approaching businesses, remember that while you may feel they owe something to the community in which they make their profits they often do not see it this way. Such an argument needs considerable political pressure to be effective. If you are approaching a businessman simply on the basis of a good idea which deserves his support and is important to his community's health, remember that most contributors like to be more involved than Santa Claus when they are giving their money away.

This does not mean that they wish to control your school, but simply that they want to be respected for their judgment (their business judgment is probably pretty good) as well as the size of their corporate purse. Simple things like asking advice and keeping contributors informed about your school may go a long way toward helping you get contributions from them in the future and from their business associates. We know of at least one case in which a local businessman gave a course in management to a school director who solicited him for funds. The course proved very helpful to the director and the school. If you pick people carefully you may be able to build some real community support.

Much of the work of raising private money involves connections— people who know people who know people who can help. You need the patience to follow up leads. Take time talking to many people, keep in touch with those who have helped, constantly try to stay on the scent. It can be a colossal drag. More things turn to ashes than to money. But if this is how you have decided to raise money, keep cool and keep hustling.

Local foundations and charities are usually small and sometimes are joined together into associations of foundations or charities. They may share one executive officer to do initial screening of proposals. If they are not joined, you may have to pick through the separate ones yourself. Before approaching these people try to find out as much as you can about how much they usually give and for what, what times of year they consider applications, what kind of supporting information they like to have. The library may have a foundation directory which will start you on this road; conversations with knowledgeable people around town (go out and look for them) will also help.

With local foundations, as with any fund raising activity, do not restrict yourself to a single description of your school as just a school. People's definitions of school are flexible; and what you are doing may be a lot more than a school. Maybe you provide social services to kids and families—you may be a multi-service center. Maybe you have a health program which can be funded separately, or a counseling program which can be attractive to those interested in community mental health, or an arts program which emphasizes "humanistic" teaching. Look at your goals and programs for things which can be funded separately. Remember that a lot of this is the art of "packaging"—making your school look unique and attractive to people whose interests you know something about. It is a little cynical, but it works.

When you get to the point of approaching large national foundations (Ford, Rockefeller, etc.), try to find out about their thinking before you make a proposal. They usually have policies about what they are currently interested in, and though you can break through this sometimes, it is best to know about them. Currently alternative schools are not terribly popular. There are hundreds and thousands of proposals from alternative schools. Foundations seem to be worried about them as endless drains which will never become self-supporting and therefore will always be asking for funds. If you can convince foundations you have a reasonable chance of becoming self-sufficient or getting public money, they will be much more interested in sustaining you while you start.

Foundations are also worried about the fact that money going to alternative schools does not affect the majority of kids who stay in public schools. If you can make a case that you are working to have an effect on the public schools, you will be in better shape. The old argument that private schools serve as models which public schools emulate because of their effectiveness is useless—largely because it simply isn't true. (You need some leverage and some aggressive tactics to change the direction of the public school juggernaut.)

Again, think freely about how to describe what you are doing. Alternative schools may be out, but "innovative curriculum development" may be in.

Be careful about being led on. Most people will tell you if you have a very slim chance, but some people wait a long time before letting the other shoe drop. Don't be afraid to ask whether you're getting serious consideration and what your chances are. Otherwise you can drain a lot of time and energy on an uncertain enterprise.

Just about every city has a few people who are experienced in raising runds from foundations and private individuals and corporations. The notes in this section are no substitute for talking with these people to find out what your best course of action is.

Self-support—Business, Contracts, Services

When you solicit funds from a foundation or an individual or a business corporation, you are essentially asking them to hand over a part of their profits to a worthy cause. This raises all the problems of having to ask for what you may feel you should be entitled to (public schools do not solicit money this way) and of justifying your values to someone else (as a matter of survival) merely because they happen to have made some money or controlled some capital. This is not entirely pleasant and raises a number of difficult political-economic questions.

It may be possible to eliminate some of this and at the same time to move toward a stable independent source of funds. To do this you may want to think about going into business yourself. We do not mean by this that schools can be run for profit (we doubt that this can be done without either exploiting the staff or cheating the students). But if your school is operating and fairly stable, you may be able to hire additional staff who would do work, at least part time, which would yield the school a profit. As an example, researchers from universities or from government agencies sometimes ask community schools to provide information about the school—to give of their experiences and the fruits of their work. Many community schools have started charging for this information. It is a very small business (which must be kept under control so you will have time left for the school) based on the fact that researchers get paid to gather this information.

The kinds of self-support you might consider could include at least:

1. *Contracts: doing work for city or state agencies.* This work would be done by people hired by you and the rate of payment would have to be high enough so that money was left over from the actual expense of doing the work to support the school. It is much better if the work itself also benefits the goals of the school. An example is The Group School, which has a contract with the local Youth Resources Bureau to run two counseling groups. One of these is for adolescents referred by the YRB (kids who are near to being in trouble with the courts) and one is run for students within The Group School. These students would want this kind of program anyway, so there is no diversion of the purposes of the school. The contract supports staff doing work the school wants done and also provides a little extra cash since the salaries of the people doing this work are higher than the amounts they actually need to get along on.

Contracts can be based on any expertise which you have or which you can acquire by hiring people who wish to be part of the community.

2. *Businesses.* It has been suggested that community schools could also go into business using the profits from the business as a means of supporting the school. We have not found any notable successes (or failures) in this area, but there have been a number of people talking about it. A number of good suggestions in this area can be found in Jonathan Kozol's book *Free Schools* in the chapter "Warehouse Bookstore: Rehab Housing: Franchise Operations." You might also look into the ideas of Charles Hampden-Turner, who has written on uses of Community Development Corporations. He can be contacted at Cambridge Institute, 1878 Massachusetts Avenue, Cambridge, Mass.

The crux of this tactic is that you become the business which you were formerly asking for money. The prospects are untested and the administrative and business expertise required to really make such an operation run successfully might prove a great obstacle. At least it should be considered. If you do get into it, be sure to get not only expert business advice, but also legal advice as to how to do this without jeopardizing your tax status with the Internal Revenue Service.

3. *Services.* This really amounts to a kind of income sharing be-

tween people who have services they can sell and the school. The school becomes a community institution with many different kinds of people associated with it. Some of these people contribute part of their pay for services they render outside the community. In exchange the community provides a certain amount of economic security by insuring at least a minimum adequate income to these people in hard times. One example is this book. It was written by some people at two community schools and the royalties will go to the support of these two schools.

The main trouble with businesses and with services is that they rely on people being willing to take less profit from their work than they can get. They are a contradiction of the entire profit motive. Yet we have seen people moving in these directions because they are committed to their schools and communities more than to their personal physical comfort and because they have come to recognize some of the social and economic drawbacks of operating on the profit motive. Many of these people believe that it would be better to change the entire economic system or at least the means of financing education, but in the meantime this is viewed as a relatively non-exploitive way to survive in the world as it is.

State Programs

It may be a considerable amount of work but it is generally worth inquiring into the state programs which might prove a source of aid to your school. You should not expect to find general school aid, but you may be able to get some money for specific purposes. Most attempts at providing general aid have foundered on the federal or state constitutional prohibitions against state support for religion. There are continued efforts to provide generalized support in accordance with constitutional requirements, most notably tax credits and tuition vouchers, but none have been successful yet.

There may be state laws in your area providing transportation or textbook loans or supplemental services (for example, health checkups) for nonpublic schools. These should be checked into.

Most states have surplus property programs, usually available through the state department of education. You are probably eligible for this program in which government surplus, from desks to dental equipment, is available for a modest handling charge (almost free). When inquiring into this, check with your lawyer if you are told you are not eligible.

Most states also administer a federal program providing free or low-cost lunches, breakfasts, and surplus foods for schools which have a large number of students from poor families. Check through your state department of education and double check any resistance you encounter with your lawyer to be sure it is legitimate.

Many states also have programs for providing supportive services for young people who have been in trouble with the courts or are near to being in such trouble. If you are careful and can find a cooperative person in such a state program you may be able to get some support if your program is helping these kids.

Once you get past these basic programs—transportation, textbooks, food, surplus property, and youth resources programs—the search becomes more difficult. Still it may be worth it. Many available programs may not be specifically for schools, but may nevertheless help you. In Massachusetts for example, a state law makes it possible for nonprofit corporations in existence for over two years to hold raffles or lotteries and keep the proceeds. There may be a welfare provision for new career training which could be used by parents learning to become teachers. Social or medical services may be available on a referral basis at local clinics or agencies and these might be useful to you. Start looking and keep looking.

Federal Programs

This is the real haystack. And there may not even be a needle in it. The same problems in aiding private schools (separation of church and state required by the Constitution) apply to federal aid as to state aid.

In addition, Congress has not seen fit to aid nonreligious private schools. This is partly because for a long time nonpublic schools were either religious (largely Catholic) or were elitist prep schools which didn't need any federal money. Perhaps if community schools become more numerous they will command enough attention to get some aid even if religious schools cannot constitutionally receive support.

It can be a hassle to apply for federal funds. Most programs have not only governing laws but administration regulations and guidelines as well. The task of fitting within these regulations can take a lot of time and things may still not work out. It also happens that the conditions of the grant can be burdensome. It is still possible, however, to get some help from the federal government. You must decide whether you really need what is offered and how much energy is going to be required to pull it off. For this reason it is advisable to work with someone who can tell you exactly what the federal program requires and then help you figure out how or whether to fit into it. A local legal service lawyer can help with this. So can some of the federal bureaucrats themselves. It is part of their job to explain to you what is required and what is available.

The following federal programs should be looked into:

Elementary and Secondary Education Act (20 U.S.C.A. 241, P.L. 89-10). ESEA is really the only large federal program of aid to education besides aid provided to "impacted areas." The funding usually goes at about the 1.5 billion dollar level, almost all of it going to public schools.

Title I. This title is for *"educationally deprived" children,* which in effect means poor children. Eligibility depends upon showing of significant numbers of children whose families earn less than $2,000/year or are on AFDC. Because of the church-state problem, private schools can participate only in "services" provided by the public school. That is, no money is actually granted to a private school, but is given to the public school in a Title I target area which then makes services available. The act states that such services are to be "special educational services and arrangements, e.g., dual enrollments, educational radio and TV, and mobile educational services." This has been known to include remedial teaching, having students as tutors, psychological testing and counseling, and special equipment. The regulations then go into considerable detail about the fact that equipment must be owned by the public schools and loaned to the private schools. Teachers (e.g., remedial reading) must be on the public payroll and visit the private school (see regs. Title 45, part 116.19a-g). The regulations can be obtained by writing to the Office of Education in Washington, or contacting the Law and Education Center at Harvard University.

The regulations (116.19b) also provide that in any program to be administered by a local education agency (public school board), there must be consultation with representatives of private schools to determine the needs of such schools and how they can participate. This usually results in consulting parochial schools but not community schools, perhaps because they are less numerous and visible. In any case, you are entitled to consultation and, if you qualify, you may get participation. Whether that participation is helpful and non-burdensome to you will depend upon the arrangement you make with the local school authorities.

It is a good idea to get some legal assistance in approaching the local school authorities for participation. You do have some rights in this matter and it is important to know both what you can demand and what depends on cooperative arrangements with school authorities so that you do not jeopardize your negotiating position. It might be possible for a group of community schools with substantial numbers of poor children enrolled to band together and have Title I pay for equipment and supplemental teachers who would be busy all the time with the community schools.

The structure of the law's administration makes the local school authorities responsible for preparing an application for Title I funds each year, with added applications for summer programs. These applications are received and processed by the State Department of Education, which at present requires that they be in at least six weeks before the program is to begin. Deadlines tend to change, though, and it is important to find out what they are. Once the state approves the local applications, the federal money is disbursed without much further ado.

There is, of course, very little reason for the Title I guidelines to be as strict as they are for nonreligious schools. There is no church-state problem involved with them. For the meantime, however, they must be lived with. We suggest that you get a copy of the latest Title I application from your local school board (you are entitled to it according to the regulations) and see whether there are any programs which you might want to participate in or whether you can think of new ones to suggest. Keep an eye open for whether community schools have been consulted as they are required to be. Check with your brother schools. If enough schools with poor children in them got it together it would probably be possible to get Title I help on good terms.

Finally, every community which has a Title I program is required by state and federal guidelines to have an advisory board elected locally. Parents and community groups are represented. You may find a sympathetic ear at the advisory board. They are probably interested in the same kinds of changes in education that you are even though their present leverage is inside the system.

Title II. This section of the act provides aid to, among others, private schools, in improving their *libraries*. The money does not depend upon the income of the families of your students, but in most states it does vary with the tax base of the area in which you are located. Library grants come in two types, the regular library improvement program and the special purpose grant. Guidelines for this program can be obtained from the Library Extension Bureau of State Department of Education.

The regular grants depend in their amount on the number of students in the private school and the present condition of the library. Per pupil the amounts are small, but there is a minimum grant of $200 so that it may be worth it even for a very small school.

You will have to show that you are a publicly certified school (see State Requirements), are willing to sign a compliance form for Title VI of the 1964 Civil Rights Act (no discrimination in use of federal funds), and are not interested in receiving books of a religious nature. Ask about the regular program and about the special purpose grants.

Title III. This section provides for innovative and experimental educational programs. Provision for participation of nonpublic schools is indicated, but we have not heard of any community school receiving substantial assistance.

Food. For the operation of federal programs providing lunch, breakfast, milk, surplus commodities, and kitchen equipment, administered by the state, see *state aid.*

Teacher Training (and Salaries?). The Manpower Development and Training Act (P.L. 87-415) may be a source of funds for training teacher aid. In a cooperative arrangement a contract would be written between the Department of Labor, which administers the act, and a community school or other institution which was willing to make teaching at the school a part of the training. As far as we have been able to find out, the chances of drawing such a contract depend almost entirely upon the particular Labor Department Field Representative you are dealing with.

Outside Chances. Another potential source of assistance in paying teacher salaries is the Career Opportunity Program of the Education Professions Development Act. If it works, the C.O.P. program will pay low-income persons including veterans to prepare for teaching jobs. Where it has been successful with community schools (very rare) the government has used the program to pay tuition at a local school of education and a stipend while the eligible persons "practice teach" at the community schools. As with most federal programs run out of the Office of Education there is need to justify the program in terms of impact on public schools. The programs are cooperative arrangements between the federal government, a local college or university, and a school.

Slightly more possible, but equally difficult to arrange, is assistance from VISTA or from the Teacher Corps. Both of these programs have uncertain futures, but might be a source of teachers or subsistence salaries for your teachers.

Finally, you might make some inquiries about the *Follow Through* program. This is a continuation of the Headstart program attempting to keep track of and help Headstart kids once they get into the first few grades of elementary school. There is one occasion in which this program was operated through a community school in Massachusetts, but the arrangement involved several other local and state agencies to such a great degree that it seems unlikely that it would happen again. Nevertheless, it may be worth inquiring into if you have some contacts with a model cities program, a state education agency, or some university.

Advice. As with all government programs, the trick is to know enough about the guidelines to be able to write your proposal so that it fits in. The other basic requirement is the proper size, shape, and number of forms and copies. Save yourself some grief if you are applying, find out all the requirements before you sit down and start writing proposals. Good luck, and remember, the government ain't likely to support alternatives to the government.

CHAPTER ELEVEN

Technical Problems: Incorporation, State Regulations, Bookkeeping, Taxation, and Insurance

Incorporation

Most alternative schools will find it advantageous to incorporate as nonprofit, educational, or charitable corporations. Forming a corporation serves two legal purposes: (1) incorporation limits the liability of the individuals involved in the school for purposes of debt collection and other damage actions; (2) more importantly, incorporation helps the school to qualify for federal tax exemption by the Internal Revenue Service as a nonprofit agency.

Incorporation also serves several nonlegal purposes. Being incorporated is one of those things which assures skeptics of the stability and acceptability of your school. If you are applying for funds someplace, trying to get a lease, or trying to get certified, it will help to be incorporated. For your own purposes, you will find that the most interesting and useful part of incorporation is in working out a form of governance for your school, and making one of many attempts to define your goals. The bylaws can be viewed as writing the first constitution of the school. There will probably be plenty of changes to be made as you go along, but at least this helps you focus initially on the question of governance and the relationship between what you need to survive in the world and the ways that you want to relate to each other inside the school.

Nonprofit corporations are chartered by the state in which they operate, and generally require both articles of incorporation and bylaws. You should check into the particular requirements in your state. In general, bylaws cover the following matters:

- name and location of office
- definition of membership and procedure for terminating membership if desired
- meetings—regular, annual, special notice requirements for meetings and quorum requirements
- board of directors—membership, election, powers, and duties and meetings of the board of directors
- committees—if necessary
- officers—titles, functions, duties, terms of office, and election and removal procedures (corporate officers usually include president, vice-president, secretary, and treasurer)
- provisions for parliamentary procedures and the corporate seal
- amendments—provisions for amending the bylaws

Bylaws may present a problem for some alternative schools. Corporate law is based on the delegation of authority to the officers and board of directors of the corporation. This may be inconsistent with a desire for a more democratic way of operating a school. Furthermore, most state corporate laws do not recognize anyone under the age of 21. This also may create a conflict between the way the state wants a corporation operated and the way you want decisions made in your school. You can avoid this by having an unofficial set of bylaws for your own use, or by setting up a responsive board of directors which can simply meet a few times a year to ratify what has been done by a more informal procedure affording greater participatory democracy. In this way, the board of directors is the official body of the corporation but the policies are really being set by the parents, teachers, and students at their own meeting. In any case, you should check your plans against the legal requirements by consulting a lawyer.

You may feel that bylaws should not be allowed to be used as a tool by anyone upset with the products of a more democratic procedure. If so, do not give either the board of directors or officers excessive power, make their removal easy, make their terms short (they can always be reelected if they are cooperative), and make it easy to loosen the bylaws through simple amendment procedures.

You can make the bylaws and corporate form respond to your needs and goals. But remember that there is always the outside chance that someone, sometime, will question whether you have a real corporation. This is especially important in applying for federal tax exemption. If you do not maintain the integrity of the corporation, individuals may be liable for something the corporation would ordinarily be liable for. Or it may jeopardize your tax exemption or make it hard for you to gain the confidence of those with whom you deal. Because of this possibility it is essential that you talk the whole matter over with a lawyer who is sympathetic to your goals. Many things can be done by you which might become evidence that your corporation does not exist (for legal purposes). You should be aware of this and always keep yourself covered.

The section on governance made reference to several issues which you will face in determining how you are to manage the affairs of your school community and its relations with others. The resolution of these questions should be expressed in the bylaws as far as possible. In drawing bylaws remember two additional things: one, there may be changes in your attitude toward the governing structure of the school or corporation and the ease of changing the bylaws should reflect how much energy you want to have to generate in order to make basic changes; two, every change you make in the bylaws should be scanned by a lawyer to be sure that it does not jeopardize the corporation or its tax exemption.

One of the most important technical aspects of getting incorporated as a nonprofit organization is making sure that your charter and bylaws are written so that it will be possible for you to get a tax exemption under section 501(c)3 of the Internal Revenue Code. This exemption is for charitable, educational, scientific and certain other nonprofit organizations. It allows contributors to your school to deduct their contributions from their income or corporate income tax and it makes it unnecessary for you to pay income tax as a corporation. Many states also follow the IRS determination in granting you tax-exempt status so you will not have to pay state sales tax on corporate purchases.

The major requirements of section 501(c)3 are that you be nonprofit and that you not engage in any political activity (as a corporation). You should be sure to have a lawyer familiar with the tax code go over your corporate papers before you file them so that he can advise you about whether you have written anything which might make it difficult to get the IRS exemption.

You should also remember when drawing up your corporate charter, which is essentially a description of your purposes and powers, that you may want to operate more than just a school. If your notion of school includes health services or parent seminars or community organizing, you should be sure that your charter uses broad enough language to enable you to do these things. The Group School, for example, is the main but not the only activity of The Group, Inc., which also runs community programs (such as counseling and training). Again, when setting up your corporation to do more than run a school as most people would think of it, be sure to have a lawyer look over the papers. Free legal help is available to those who qualify under poverty guidelines. Consult a local legal services office or OEO Office for this.

State Requirements

The regulation of private schools in most states leaves considerable discretion to state or local authorities. While the statutes may appear to make it fairly easy to establish a nonpublic school, the absence of firm rights for nonpublic schools and the unpredictability of the enforcement of the laws could at any time generate considerable insecurity for nonpublic schools. Discretionary authority can be the mother of flexibility or repression, depending on the political atmosphere.

A substantial increase in the number of nonpublic schools will probably lead to increased investigation and regulation. Doing your political groundwork, therefore, will probably be as important as knowing the legal requirements which affect you. In reading through this section keep in mind that it is your own educational standards which are most important. The basic decisions described in earlier sections should be reached before you concern yourself in detail with the legal requirements.

You should keep in mind also that while the state may make reasonable requirements designed to secure a basic minimum education to all students required to attend school, it may not compel anyone to attend public schools or so regulate private schools as to make them identical to public schools. (For support of this notion, see the Supreme Court case *Pierce v. Society of Sisters,* 268 US 510.)

State requirements for nonpublic schools come in many sizes and colors. It is a subject which you can learn about by consulting other community schools in your area and by asking a lawyer for a rundown of the requirements and the way they are enforced. The basic requirement is that a nonpublic school be certified or approved as a legal alternative to the public schools. Until this is done, students of compulsory school age who attend your school instead of a public school or another certified school, will be considered truant and they or their parents may be subject to legal action, fines, etc. The school may also get into trouble for encouraging truancy if the state has a law covering this. You should check into this in detail before enrolling any students.

The power to approve or certify a school for children of compulsory school age rests either with the state (usually the department of education) or with the local school authorities. Some states have statutes which set out specifically what the requirements are and what process has been established to insure that applicants get a fair decision. But many states are still operating under vague laws and many have no procedures at all. Some do not even have standards. This vagueness can mean that getting certified is essentially a political matter. You should check into the requirements and also the reality of how the system works.

Certification or approval is not the same as accreditation in most places. There are private associations which examine schools and then give them a stamp of approval. This quality judgment (at least according to someone's definition of quality) is called accreditation and almost never has any legal significance. There are those who claim that it helps when school graduates are applying to college and that this form of private regulation forestalls more rigorous examination by state governments. We leave it to someone else to determine whether this is so. In general these associations can be found by getting in touch with the National Association of Independent Schools in Boston.

The requirements which the *state* imposes as a condition of getting certified usually include something on each of the following subjects:

- curriculum requirements—certain courses may be required to be offered or taught
- teacher qualifications—some states require that teachers in non-public schools be certified
- records—most states require that attendance records and other information about students be kept by the school
- testing—some states have begun to require that all students take standardized tests in basic skills
- hours and days—the state may require a certain number of hours per day or days per year of school
- purposes and programs—some states require that you submit a description of your educational goals and your program

In administering these educational requirements the state may have the power to come and inspect the school from time to time.

In addition to educational requirements, you will have to meet building codes and fire, health, and safety requirements. Each of these is complex and difficult to understand. Some parts are plainly for the protection of the students and staff. Others seem more remote. The way that the code is administered varies tremendously from state to state. There are also local codes which have to be met in most places. In general, it is a good idea to try to establish some kind of friendly relationship with the inspectors and to ask them about the requirements for any particular building which you may be thinking of using. Some schools have gotten stuck with enormous renovation bills because they did not discover that their building had code violations until after they had moved in.

Often it is hard to get any building approved as a school. For this reason you may want to consider the possibility of using some building which has already been approved (such as an abandoned Catholic school). In any case, getting by the codes can become an extremely political matter in some places. Be sure that you understand the way the system works before you begin dealing with it. The best source of information is probably other community schools and the inspectors themselves.

Some state departments of education have compilations of the requirements which are made of nonpublic schools. For a fairly detailed example of all state regulations (for Massachusetts) write to the Center for Law and Education, 38 Kirkland Street, Cambridge, 02138 and ask for a free copy of "Alternative Schools: A Practical Manual."

Bookkeeping

No matter how little or how much money you have, it is absolutely essential to keep careful records of what comes in and what goes out. In addition, there are some state and federal forms which you must fill out periodically. All of this is essential to retain your tax-exempt status, to prevent anyone from questioning the validity of your corporation, and to protect you from charges of misuse of any funds you receive.

Forms

1. *SS-4.* This is the application for a federal Employer Identification Number. It is necessary for withholding taxes and to attain tax-exempt status.
2. *W-4.* This is the form which employees fill out stating the number of exemptions they claim. It is the basis for calculating the withholding tax from their salaries.
3. *941.* This is the quarterly tax report. As a tax-exempt organization you will not pay any taxes to the United States, but you do have to report salaries paid, and the withholding from those salaries is then paid to the IRS on a quarterly basis. If your withholding reaches a certain level, or if you otherwise desire, you make monthly withholding "deposits" instead of quarterly payments. This is taken care of with form *501* monthly and *941* quarterly. Your bank will be involved in this process.
4. *W-2.* This is the year-end report of withholding which you must file with the IRS and the individual staff person.
5. If you are interested in Social Security, ask the IRS for form *SS-15* and *SS-15a*. This comes to about 9% tax, half from the school, half from the employee's paycheck.
6. Your state government will also have tax and other forms. Check into it.

Accounts

Bookkeeping need only be understandable and accurate. As long as the system you use tells you exactly how much you take in and from whom, when and on what money is spent, and maintains receipts, you will probably be in good shape. Make sure the system has some permanence and is kept up to date. An accountant's book is helpful and not terribly expensive. At the end of each accounting year, have your books audited. It's for your protection.

Remember that anything you show as being received (or which you give a donor evidence of having received) must be accounted for. All money for which you give receipts must be accounted for as expenditures or as money still in the bank. If a donor asks for a receipt (for example, to prove his contribution is tax deductible on his own return), give him one and be sure to record the donation in your books. The dates and purposes and amounts of all expenditures (rent, supplies, utilities, transportation, etc.) should be recorded.

The books should record all payments to staff under the staff person's name, and the receipt of tuition if there is any. If you should receive either a federal, state, or private grant or contract, keep separate books for this so that you will be able to show them what you did with the money.

If your books are confusing or aren't working, get some professional help. Don't bumble along; accounting help can probably be gotten free someplace. Look around.

Some banks give charge-free checking accounts to nonprofit organizations. Make some calls and you'll find one that does.

Federal Tax Exemption

Soon after you have incorporated you will want to file with the federal government for tax-exempt status. This will eliminate the necessity for the school to pay taxes and it will make contributions to you tax deductible for donors. Employees will still have to pay income tax.

To gain your exemption, file form 1023 with the Internal Revenue Service. You can get it from your district IRS Office along with Circular E which provides some help in filling out the form. To qualify you must satisfy the IRS that you are an educational or charitable nonprofit institution which does not engage in political activity designed to influence legislation or election campaigns. The form requires considerably detailed information about your organization and its operation and finances as well as copies of articles of incorporation, bylaws, books, etc. You should be sure that this form is answered by a lawyer since there are some pitfalls and the application process can be drawn out considerably if you need to make changes.

Since your incorporation and early activities will influence your ability to get tax-exempt status, you should discuss these matters early and avoid mistakes. Once you have filed it will take several months for the IRS to send you a letter confirming your exemption. When you have received this letter it usually will help you in getting tax-exempt status on the state level, since most states accept the federal determination for purposes of state tax exemptions.

Insurance

As individuals or as a nonprofit corporation running a school you will want to protect yourselves against lawsuits and your students against medical expenses arising out of accidents occurring in connection with school activities. You should have some form of agreement or permission slip signed by parents of students indicating that they approve of their children's attendance there. In addition, there are several types of insurance which can be arranged at a relatively low cost. Some of these plans include:

1. liability insurance for the building in which the school is located, covering bodily injury and property damage.
2. group accident insurance covering medical expenses up to $1000 and life insurance to $10,000. This is a benefit to the school greater than just protection from suits, since many people would have to pay higher rates for such coverage individually.
3. automobile insurance specifically covering student passengers. The laws in your state covering "school buses" and transportation of students should be checked carefully. Insurance may be expensive but necessary.
4. workman's compensation plans may be available to you de-

pending on your circumstances and whether staff get paid.

5. comprehensive general liability insurance will protect both the premises and other named or unnamed places you use as part of the school program.

There are other policies, including fire and theft insurance, and the ones which are needed or available depend on the specific circumstances of your school.

Permission Slips. In addition to whatever insurance arrangements you make, you should contact a lawyer with regard to the wording of permission slips and other agreements of parents regarding attendance at your school.

It is advisable and in some places absolutely necessary that you obtain medical release forms for all students as a protective measure. These should be kept on file and be available on field trips in case of accident.

CHAPTER TWELVE

Resources: People and Things

Goals and Purposes

Summerhill, A Radical Approach to Child Rearing. A.S. Neill, Hart, $2.45. The granddaddy of all "free school" books. It might seem unnecessary to mention this book, as it has become so widely known, but for many of us, *Summerhill* has been the strongest written influence on the shaping of our educational ideas.

De-Schooling Society, Ivan Illich, Harper & Row, $5.95. This book expounds the author's theory that "for most men the right to learn is curtailed by the obligation to attend school." Illich attempts to establish some criteria for what sorts of institutions actually foster learning.

Teacher, Sylvia Ashton-Warner, Bantam, $1.25. An exciting and well-written account of one teacher's experience teaching reading, and a description of the method she devised. Sylvia Ashton-Warner was teaching Maori children in New Zealand, but her experiences and method are entirely relevant to more familiar elementary school situations.

The Lives of Children, George Dennison, Vintage, $1.95. This is an interesting journal of the highlights of a year in a community school. A number of poeple have had their thinking straightened out by this insightful description of a school without bureaucracy. There is a chapter containing practical suggestions learned by those involved in the First Street School.

Schools Where Children Learn, Joseph Featherstone, Liveright, $2.45. An eye-witness report on how several American schools have adopted and modified the British infant school model.

The Student as Nigger, Jerry Farber, Pocket Books, $.95. A brief and excellent analysis of the values that underlie traditional classroom structures and of how these structures socialize students into docile, obedient, dependent individuals. One of the more famous writings to come from the campus educational reform movement, it is equally relevant to high school and elementary school situations.

How Children Fail, John Holt, Dell, $.95. This is about how public schools keep kids from thinking, with good suggestions of ways to reverse this trend in traditional classroom structures.

The Montessori Method, Maria Montessori, Schocken, $1.95. A good general description and background to the Montessori approach. Clear descriptions of materials, and lots of practical advice on how to use them. She also explains much of the thinking that led to various aspects of her approach.

The Language and Thought of the Child, Jean Piaget, Meridian, $1.45. Piaget is a pretty significant man in the general field of child development, and this is probably the best book of his with regard to schools. It discusses the significance of different language patterns in children between the ages of 4 and 11, and how these relate to the development of the child.

Toward a Theory of Instruction, Jerome Bruner, Harvard University Press, $4.50. *The Process of Education,* Jerome Bruner, Vintage, $1.35. These two books have been recommended to us as good examples of Bruner's thought. His theory is that with the right kind of teaching, and given time, anybody can learn anything (almost). He argues that intelligence is not what determines how much a person can learn.

Experience and Education, John Dewey, Collier, $.95. This is a lecture series in which Dewey summarizes his views on teaching methods, basically in response to critics. He was a pioneer in progressive education, one of the first to talk about "learning by doing."

Day School E.P.A., Recipe for Building a School, Facts About the Nairobi School, available from Nairobi Day School, P.O. Box 10777, Palo Alto, California 94303. These are three good pamphlets put out by the Nairobi Schools, whose special emphasis is on the needs of people of color. *Day School E.P.A.* is a graphic account of the events that led to the decision to start the Nairobi Schools, and what followed from that. *Recipe for Building a School* is just that. *Facts*

About the Nairobi School is a description of what the schools are trying to do.

The Pedagogy of the Oppressed, Paolo Friere, Herder and Herder, $5.95. This book is really dense and hard to read, but Friere has developed some interesting ways of working with people, so you may find it worth wading through. His general focus is on getting people to name for themselves the most important themes in their lives, rather than having outsiders tell them what is important. From this concept, specific curricula can be developed. People who find Friere interesting may be interested in contacting Michael Sherwin (5933 Pulaski Avenue, Germantown, Pa.) who has worked to apply Friere's method to his own learning and that of people around him.

Teaching as a Subversive Activity, Postman & Weingarten, Delacorte, $2.25. This is based on the idea that "our present educational system is not viable and is certainly not capable of generating enough energy to lead its own revitalization." The authors give practical suggestions on how to educate for change.

Free Schools, Jonathan Kozol, Houghton-Mifflin, $4.95. An articulate book for those whose idea of free school is that it is not relevant to the urban poor. It might straighten you out if you think freedom and escape are identical. It contains some practical information and has a good resource listing.

Parents

How to Change the Schools, A Parents' Action Handbook on How to Fight the System, Ellen Lurie, Random House, $2.95. Written by the mother of five children, this is a catalog of what she's learned in 15 years of trying to make the public schools good enough for her kids. It contains an extensive bibliography especially relevant to New York City.

Afram Associates, 68 East 131 Street, New York, N.Y. 10037; telephone: (212) 690-7010. Afram Associates maintain both library services and consulting teams. Their emphasis is on the Black community, and education is only one of their concerns. Their Action Library disseminates information on action and position statements that cover a broad variety of issues. This subscription service includes articles, bibliographies, fact sheets, films, and tapes. Educational inquiries should go to Preston Wilcox, the executive director; library inquiries to Annette Ramsey.

East Harlem Block Schools, 94 East 111 Street, New York, N. Y. 10029. These folks see part of their task as helping other groups of parents learn from the East Harlem experience. They're happy to have visitors and run a kind of informal consulting service.

Nairobi Day School, P.O. Box 10777, Palo Alto, California 94313; telephone: (415) 325-4049. Nairobi Day School has organized a consulting team to work with other people starting new schools. Nairobi is a predominantly black elementary school that is working carefully to develop programs that address the particular needs of people of color. The school is in close association with Nairobi High School and Nairobi College. Together the schools' consulting teams help people who are developing similar programs. The schools use this service as a source of income. Special financial arrangements may be possible for community groups.

Curriculum

Reading in the Elementary School, Jeannette Veatch, Ronald, $7.00. A traditional text, but a good one, that covers many different techniques for individualized teaching of reading. It is especially useful for the teaching of beginning reading.

Citation Press Series: British Infant Schools, Citation Press, 50 West 44 Street, New York, N.Y.; telephone: (212) 867-7700. This is a series of 13 paperbound books, ranging in price from $.95 to $2.95. In the series, a number of authors examine various aspects of open education as practiced in British elementary schools. Publication was begun in late 1971, and by Spring of '72 a total of 23 titles and a cumulative volume will be available.

Teacher, Sylvia Ashton-Warner, Bantam, $1.25. See the annotation under Goals and Purposes.

Big Rock Candy Mountain, Portola Institute, 1115 Merrill Street, Menlo Park, California. This quarterly deals with education in general; each particular edition has its own theme. Especially useful is the Education and Classroom Materials issue, complete with articles on materials, list of suppliers, and a letter from John Holt discussing some good recent books on education. BRCM is like a Whole Earth Catalog on education, if that makes anything clearer.

What We Owe Children, The Subordination of Teaching to Learning, Dr. Caleb Gattegno, Avon, $1.65. Gattegno was impressed by the intellectual powers implied by a child's learning a language by the age of two or so. This book discusses how we can help children learn by linking new knowledge to what they already know.

Educational Solutions, Inc., Box 190, Cooper Station, New York, N. Y. 10003, Dr. Caleb Gattegno, director. Formerly called Schools for the Future, this consulting service runs workshops for teachers and parents. The East Harlem Block Schools found them to provide "the most clearcut, disciplined insight into how kids can be challenged. The stuff can demonstrate what it feels like to be incredibly smart and learn new skills very rapidly." They run practical workshops on how to teach reading, math, and foreign languages. The western branch is at 77 Mark Drive, Northgate Industrial Park, San Rafael, California 94903.

SRA Kits, Science Research Associates, 259 E. Erie Street, Chicago, Illinois 60611. Elaborate and "scientifically developed," these color-coded gadgetted kits can be useful in working with kids in such areas as spelling, math, and science. They are very famous. Our experience with them has been some good and some bad, depending on how interested the kids are in things like spelling, math, and elaborate color-coded kits.

The Montessori Method, Maria Montessori, Schocken, $1.95. See annotation under Goals and Purposes.

Montessori's Own Handbook, Maria Montessori, Schocken, $1.75. A concise handbook particularly designed for parents. It illustrates many of the materials and their uses. Less theory than *The Montessori Method.*

Far West Laboratory for Educational Research and Development, 1 Garden Circle, Hotel Claremont, Berkeley, California 94705; telephone: (415) 841-9710. Far West Labs is a public nonprofit laboratory that deals with the inventing, designing, developing, and testing of educational products. It tries to promote the use of these products in the classroom and in teacher training. Five primary areas of concern are: early childhood education; teacher education; multi-ethnic education; utilization and information; and communications. Visitors are welcome. For further information contact Margaret Jones at the above address.

Children Come First, Casey and Liza Murrow, American Heritage. This is an excellent description of life in the British primary schools. Very concrete and yet perceptive.

Educational Development Center, 55 Chapel Street, Newton, Massachusetts 02160. EDC offers a wide variety of workshops for teachers and is often an excellent inexpensive source of materials for use both in and out of the classroom. Materials also include films and pamphlets on learning, curricula, and innovative schools.

Nairobi Day School, P.O. Box 10777, Palo Alto, California 94303; telephone: (415) 325-4049. Nairobi Day School has developed an elaborate curriculum that focuses on the particular interest of people of color, and there don't seem to be very many such curricular models around. They are marketing their curriculum as a way of supporting their school. It's available from them exclusively.

Deganawidah-Quetzalcoatl University(!), P.O. Box 409, Davis, California 95616; telephone: (916) 758-0470. This is a university that started in July, 1971, with emphasis on the culture and traditions of Chicano and Native American people. It is an accredited university and is anxious to help other schools develop similar programs. The executive director there is José de la Isla.

Schools Without Failure, William Glasser, M.D., Harper & Row, $4.95. This book analyzes the elements of the educational system which build in failure for many students. Glasser offers many practical suggestions on how to make a school more relevant, and thus more exciting, for everyone.

Montessori—A Modern Approach, Paula Polk Lillard, Schocken Books, New York. A good overview and introduction to the Montessori method. Ties together the origin and history of Montessori with its modern practice.

Understanding Children's Play, Ruth Hartley, Lawrence Frank; Columbia University Press. A classic, about 300 pages, lots of good theory and anecdotes, basic for early childhood.

Behavior and Misbehavior, James L. Hymes, Jr., Prentice-Hall, Englewood Cliffs, New Jersey, $1.95. Easy, fast reading, fun, to the point, very helpful when you've given up.

The Logic of Action, Francis Pockman Hawkins, Elementary Science Advisory Center, University of Colorado, $1.95. Interesting anecdotal description of a year's work in an open activity program with deaf children; good comments on teacher's role and lots of detail on materials used. Probably have to write to the University of Colorado to get it. 150 pages.

The Magic Years, Selma Fraiberg, Scribner, $2.45. Useful for parents and teachers. Basic and human description of child development from birth through age six.

Water, Sand, and Mud as Play Materials, pamphlet from National Association for Nursery Education, 155 East Ohio Street, Chicago, Illinois, $.50. Short, sweet, a very good way to validate the joys of mess and the learning opportunities of mess!

The Balance Book, E.S.S., Educational Services Inc. The address given in the book is Box 415, Watertown, Mass. 02172, 147 pages. A full, detailed, concrete guide to all the possibilities for using and studying the principle of balance, with many different materials. For young children—nursery through early primary.

Light and Shadows, E.S.S., Webster Division, McGraw-Hill. Short, pictures, quick transmission of interesting, concrete ideas.

Attribute Games and Problems, E.S.S., Webster Division, McGraw-Hill. Many concrete ideas and directions for math and other logical-thinking games. 87 pages.

Talks for Primary Teachers, Madeleine Goutard, Educational Solutions Inc., Broadway and 12th Street, New York. Short, pithy, theoretical guide to the use of Cuisenaire Rods according to the pure math of the authors of the method. A bible for people really into math teaching by rods.

What Is Music for Young Children?, Elizabeth Jones, National Association for the Education of Young Children, Washington, D.C. Anecdotal and suggestive description of music in nursery schools, encouraging experimentation, $1. Can be ordered from Publications Dept., NAEYC, 1834 Connecticut Ave., N.W., Washington, D.C. 20009.

Staff

The Teacher Paper, 280 North Pacific Avenue, Monmouth, Oregon 97361. A periodical that presents experiences of teachers in various situations: successes, failures, problems. The paper avoids the usual professional jargon. We haven't seen the paper ourselves, but we've heard good things about it from several different people.

Anger and the Rocking Chair, Janet Lederman, McGraw-Hill, $4.95. A book that focuses on the use of Gestalt Therapy techniques and perspective with elementary school children. A good source of inspiration for discouraged teachers.

Behavior and Misbehavior, J. Hymes, Prentice-Hall, $2.95. A short, simple book that can be read in a couple of hours before bed on the most frustrating day of the year and let you wake up the next morning ready to try again. Talks about why kids become "discipline problems" and how to deal with them.

General

New Schools Exchange, 701B Anacapa, Santa Barbara, California 93101; telephone: (805) 962-2020. If you want to know about schools, books, or clearinghouses, this is a decent place to start. The New Schools Exchange has been operating for three years. It serves as a national clearinghouse for alternative education though in the past it has not been particularly strong on the problems of schools in the Black and Third World communities. Twice a month, the exchange publishes a newsletter, including articles by well-known writers in education as well as profiles of schools. In 1970, the Exchange published a directory of alternative schools throughout the country. Newsletter #61 is a supplement to the directory. Also particularly useful are newsletters #55 (a bibliography) and #65 (a list of clearinghouses).

Shasta School, 499 Alabama Street, San Francisco, California. Shasta School was initiated by four students who were unhappy with their public school and decided they could do better. They did. The school is run entirely by its students. People there would be very helpful to other groups of students interested in initiating schools. If you have any doubts about whether students can really start and run a school you ought to get in touch with them and show yourself otherwise.

Inside Summerhill, Joshua Popenoe, Hart, $1.95. Written by a student at Summerhill, it gives an insider's view of the joys and sorrows of that particular institution. A very enjoyable example of how students view their schools. Popenoe also did the excellent photography.

New Schools: A National Directory, October, 1971. Available from Ralph Sama, 1878 Massachusetts Ave., Cambridge, Mass. This is the most up-to-date listing we have seen. It contains information about the composition, size, finances, and outstanding characteristics of each school listed, as well as a bibliography and a listing of 24 "coordinating and information centers" around the country.

Teacher Drop-Out Center, University of Massachusetts, Amherst, Massachusetts. Serves as a clearinghouse for information about education and particularly about available jobs in alternative schools. Sympathetic and attentive to teachers dissatisfied with the public school system.

Summerhill Society of California, P.O. Box 2477, Van Nuys, California 91401. This groups offers conferences, workshops, and films for people interested in Summerhillian educational ideas. In addition, the Society publishes a bulletin, a book list, and a list of Summerhillian schools in the western United States.

Alternatives for Education, 1778 S. Holt Ave., Los Angeles, California 90035; telephone: (213) 839-6994. Emphasizing Southern California, this group deals with a wide range of alternatives. They have a daily radio show, a monthly newsletter, a book list, and a list of day schools. The group is energetic, dedicated, and friendly.

Modern Play School, Play Mountain Place, 6063 Hargis, Los Angeles, California; telephone: (213) 870-4381. One of the oldest "Summerhillian" schools in the country (23 years), the school is interested in helping others start. Workshops in non-authoritarian teaching are available to any group of 15 interested people.

Summerhill Collective, 137 West 14 Street, New York, N.Y. 10011. The Collective is a split-off from the New York Summerhill Society. It emphasizes its collective nature and is particularly concerned with organizing for youth liberation. A newsletter is available.

Regional and National Clearinghouses. Following are a *few* of the places throughout the country interested in disseminating information on existing alternatives, starting schools, changes within public schools. Regardless of your location or the type of school you want to start, there is a clearinghouse nearby to help you. If no nearby group is listed here, it can be located by contacting New Schools Exchange (see page 134) or looking in *New Schools: A National Directory* (see page 135).

Wisconsin Coalition for Educational Reform, 3019 N. Farwell Avenue, Milwaukee, Wisconsin 53211. The Wisconsin Coalition, working throughout the state, is interested both in alternatives and in organizing for reform within the state educational system. The group offers information, for example, on legal means of dealing with inequities in the public high schools.

New Schools Movement, Earth Station 7, 402 15th Street, East, Seattle, Washington 98102. *Center for Urban Education,* same address. These two groups, originally one, have recently split. The New Schools Movement deals primarily with free schools and aims at establishing the best possible independent alternatives. The Center for Urban Education is concerned mainly with alternatives possible within the system and concentrates on organization and development of educational tactics to change the existing educational scheme.

KOA, Goddard College, Plainfield, Vermont. One of the most radically coalition-oriented groups on the east coat. Also write c/o Arrakis, RFD #1, Jeffersonville, New York.

New Schools News, c/o Bea Gillette, 407 South Dearborn, Chicago, Illinois. New Schools News is an information service for alternative schools in the Chicago area. Special attention is given to students seeking alternatives. The service operates with the cooperation of the American Friends Service Committee.

New Schools Network, 3039 Deakin, Berkeley, California 94705. The Network serves as a clearinghouse for both public and private alternative schools in the Berkeley area. It helps both parents and students looking for schools and teachers and volunteers looking for jobs through listings in its newsletter.

Federation of Boston Community Schools. Ann Pettit, 76 Highland Street, Roxbury, Massachusetts. A loose affiliation of community schools serving the Black community in the Boston area.

Federation of Independent Community Schools, 2637 North 11 Street, Milwaukee, Wisconsin 53206. These seven schools used to be Catholic schools in Milwaukee. Instead of closing the schools outright, the church turned them over to community groups. The director there is Jesse Wray.

National Association of Community Schools, c/o Don Stocks, 1707 N Street, N.W., Washington, D.C. Just beginning as a resource for community schools.

Education Switchboards. A number of education switchboards have been established as clearinghouses for information on new schools. Their general function is to put interested schools, teachers, students, and parents in touch with each other and to help get the word around that new schools exist. If there are many new schools in your area, there's probably a switchboard. Try to find it. They generally are in touch with a wide variety of situations and people.

Vocations for Social Change, Box 13, Canyon, California 94516. This is a collective that publishes a bi-monthly newsletter directed toward people who are redefining their sense of work, money, and style of life. They have centers in various parts of the country, and if there's one near you, it would be worth going to talk to people there about new schools. They're usually well grounded in what's going on in their part of the world. The current representatives are listed in each issue of the VSC newsletter, which is published in Canyon.

Clearinghouse, Department of Education, University of Massachusetts, Amherst, Massachusetts 01002. This innovative project was established to serve people who are exploring innovative learning environments. They've had their problems, but should have good information on what's going on.

Educational Confederation of Metropolitan St. Louis, 5555 Page, St. Louis, Missouri. The Confederation consists of a mixture of types of schools, some community-based, some free, some traditional private schools. Several of the schools in the Confederation are investigating the possibilities of becoming part of the public school system.

Other clearinghouses:

Teachers Organization Project and *Chicago Teaching Center,* 852 W. Belmont Avenue, Chicago, Illinois.

Washington Area Free Schools Clearing House, 1609 19th Street, N.W., Washington, D. C. 20009.

New Jersey Alternative Schools, c/o Terry Ripmaster, 16 Crestwood Drive, Glen Rock, N. J.

Innovative Education Coalition, 1130 N. Ramparts St., New Orleans, Louisiana 70116.

Southwest Education Reform Committee (SWERC) (!) 3505 Main Street, Houston, Texas 77002.

Center for Student Citizenship, Rights & Responsibilities, 1145 Germantown St., Dayton, Ohio 45408.

This Magazine is About Schools, 56 Esplanade St. East, Suite 301, Toronto 215, Ontario, Canada. A quarterly journal on educational issues, both theoretical and practical. It is published by a group of Canadians who work in and around Toronto. This Mag has recently moved away from a concentration on free schools and is now helping to promote and facilitate community control of public schools.

Center for New Schools, 431 S. Dearborn, Room 1527, Chicago, Illinois 60605; telephone: (312) 922-7436. The Center, a nonprofit corporation, aims at developing a technical assistance group to help schools in the Midwest, primarily those within the public system. Originally part of the Urban Research Corporation, the organization helped to start Metro High School, a school without walls within the Chicago public school system. The Center for New Schools consults with community groups, state educational agencies, and school staffs. Two publications are available, both relevant to starting schools: *The Metro School: A Report on the Progress of Chicago's Experimental School Without Walls,* $2.50; *Student Involvement in Decision-Making in an Alternative High School,* $6.00.

Affective Education Development Program, Norman Newberg, c/o Philadelphia Public Schools. Papers are available discussing various philosophies which might lead to the starting of new schools.

New Nation Seed Fund, Box 4026, Philadelphia, Pennsylvania 19118. A small fund to help new schools through emergencies.

Technical Problems

Legal Services Offices (OEO). Most areas are serviced by an LSO which provides free legal help to those who qualify under poverty guidelines. Good especially for incorporation, tax certification.

Volunteers in Technical Assistance (VITA). A bank of technical consultants (free to you) which has local offices in many cities. Poverty criteria apply. National office is VITA-USA, College Campus,

Schenectady, New York 12308. Harvey Pressman, VITA, 115 Gainsborough Street, Boston, Massachusetts 02115 is especially experienced in helping schools nationwide.

Alternative Schools: A Practical Manual. Available from Law & Education Center, 38 Kirkland Street, Cambridge, Massachusetts. An example of a full description of legal requirements and available government resources (for Massachusetts only).

No More Public School, by Hal Bennett, Random House. A detailed review of California's legal standards for nonpublic schools, private tutoring, and other legal alternatives to public school. Also contains suggestions about curriculum, materials, and teaching.

Afterword

A Case For Parent Control
by Dorothy Stoneman

Community control of schools has many advocates, most of them members of the community that wants to gain control. Their analysis of why community control is essential is basically a political one, seeing the school as a colonial institution that reflects and perpetuates our society's oppression of minority groups. Community control to some represents an opportunity for oppressed Black and Hispanic people to hook into political power, gaining control of a central institution; to others it is simply and wholly a way to reclaim the parental right of providing for your children's future.

The opponents of community control have been, for the most part, professional educators on the one hand and legislators on the other. They insist that poor people are not qualified to run the schools; they imply that poor people in power would be corrupt and torn by violent power-struggles; they insist that the impulse behind the struggle for control is a desire for jobs or for power, not an interest in the children. It is not difficult to understand why educators and legislators see community control as a threat to jobs and power.

As a professional educator convinced not only of the political need for community control but of its superiority as a structure for an educational institution, I'd like to present a theoretical and educational defense of community control.

For simplicity, I will talk about a parent-controlled school, rather than a community-controlled school. In the best of all political systems I believe there would be no essential difference. In America, where we are raised to take care only of our own, the general population of any community cannot be trusted to look out for some people's children as well as the people themselves can be trusted. Also, where routes to power are limited and competition intense, in a country that condones selfish uses of power, it is best to exclude from power those people who have no immediate and personal interest in the quality of the school as it affects their own children. Of course, in saying this I immediately alienate that minority of people who favor community control as a stepping-stone to political power. That's okay. My argument is not that community control is a necessary part of the political revolution. It is that parent control is a necessary part of the education revolution.

My argument is based on the following assumptions:

1. That schools for minority children run and staffed by people of the white majority have failed.

2. That members of the white majority cannot free themselves from racist and class attitudes they have been taught unless the power relationship between them and the minority group is dramatically changed.

3. That members of minority groups cannot free themselves from the racist and class ideas they have been taught unless the power relationship between themselves and the white majority with whom they come in contact is dramatically changed.

4. That children cannot get a good education in an environment where adults are divided by racist and class attitudes.

5. That racist and class attitudes are often as much a problem between nonwhite professionals and parents of poor children as they are between white professionals and the same parents. Therefore the problem of these attitudes and their effect on the children cannot be solved simply by hiring more minority-group professional educators. Professionalism is itself a class attitude, and often includes racist overtones, regardless of the professional's race.

6. That a good education for children includes the development of pride, hope, responsibility, the expectation of growing into a fulfilling adult life within a community, and the motivation to use opportunities for growing.

7. That in a ghetto area the only kind of school which has the possibility of developing these attitudes and feelings is one which is

itself a responsible and cooperative community within which a child's parents have an opportunity for a fulfilling adult life, for pride, hope, responsibility, and for personal growth.

8. That the only kind of school offering this opportunity to parents is one in which the parents have primary responsibility for the operation, development, and direction of the school.

9. That a child's identification with his parents and with his own community is a more important determinant of his expectations than any particular school experience.

10. That the best school will combine an opportunity for the student to respect and identify with his own community and an opportunity to master the skills of the dominant culture.

11. That a school presenting skills and mastery as a means to separate oneself from one's own community is destructive of a community's development.

12. That a community's development is more important to all the children residing within it than is the provision of an escape route for a small minority of a community's children.

13. That only a parent-controlled community school has the possibility of providing community identification and relationships along with academic skills and mastery.

14. That professional teachers tend to forgive themselves for not succeeding fully at their job because their job is so very difficult.

15. That, having forgiven themselves and needing still further justification for their failure, professional teachers tend to blame parents for the failures of children in their classes.

16. That this defensive process of externalizing the causes for failure tends to exacerbate racist and class attitudes, tends to create a self-fulfilling prophecy for the performance of some children, and tends toward an ever-decreasing effort on the part of the teacher.

17. That this defensive process of externalizing also acts as reassurance to the teacher that he deserves to keep his job regardless of the results of his work.

18. That the only way to cut through this defensive process is to make the teacher accountable precisely to the group of people he tends to blame for his own failure. His defensiveness can no longer be a source of reassurance concerning his job security; it will become a

source of insecurity and there will therefore be pressure on him to stop blaming the parents.

19. That only if a teacher is not blaming parents for a child's failure is a teacher in a position to work creatively with parents to insure a child's success.

20. That parents in a position to hire and fire teachers, as in a parent-controlled school, will not tolerate teacher failure and will not tolerate being blamed for teacher failure.

21. That this refusal to tolerate failure will generate in teachers a new commitment to success.

22. That this commitment to success will be accompanied not by blaming parents, since this is not to be tolerated, but by a willingness to cooperate with parents.

23. That cooperation between parents and teachers is inherently better for the educational process than mutual suspicion, contempt, accusation, or fear.

24. That teachers tend, also in a defensive process of justifying their own failure or their own limited success, to divide their classes mentally into those children they consider reachable and those children they consider unreachable. They forgive themselves more easily for not reaching the "unreachables."

25. That parents as a group will not tolerate a teacher's blame of any parents nor the dismissal of any child as incorrigible or uneducable. This group pressure on the teacher will prevent the teacher from mentally dividing his class into the educable and the non-educable.

26. That a school that refuses to consider any child unreachable is a better community for all the children.

27. That a school that is accountable to parents is less likely to consider any child unreachable.

Appendix

The Schools

The Learning Place is an alternative junior and senior high school in San Francisco, founded in 1969. Its purpose is to help its members develop the emotional strength and personal skills necessary to forge individual and collective alternatives to working class and middle class life styles. The student body of 60 is racially and ethnically mixed but predominantly white working and middle class in origin. Founded by four teachers, the school is presently governed by all-school meetings and committees having student majorities. The school is supported by a sliding scale tuition and by fundraising projects of parents, students, and staff. The parents have given active support to the school, though they play no formal role in its governance. The school operates in the Summerhillian tradition of allowing students virtually free choice of how they spend their time and use the school's resources.

The East Harlem Block Schools are a complex of parent-controlled day care centers, a tutoring program, and an elementary school in a poor, predominantly Puerto Rican section of New York City. The elementary school was founded in 1967 and now enrolls 110 students. Parents hold all positions on governing boards and committees and fill a majority of staff positions as well. The educational program is open and innovative, but places a high priority on giving children the academic and other skills which the parents consider necessary for survival. The school is open to any child in the neighborhood, free of tuition, and is supported by government grants and contributions of foundations and individual benefactors.

Presidio Hill School is a progressive school in San Francisco founded more than 50 years ago. Its primarily middle class, but racial-

145

ly integrated, student body of more than 200 is drawn from through-out the city. Most of the students are in the equivalent of grades one through six, but a junior high school was recently established. The school is legally a parent cooperative, supported entirely by tuition, with a governing board of parents and staff elected by an annual meeting. The educational program is in the tradition of John Dewey and has recently been influenced by the British infant schools.

The Berkeley Montessori School in Berkeley, California, is 8 years old and enrolls more than one hundred students from mostly white middle class families. It is run collectively by the teaching staff with the active support and cooperation of the parents. The structure and curriculum are based on Montessori methods and materials, but the staff has adapted them to the particular community and group of students. It features a unique outdoor classroom, staffed and available to children all day long. It is supported entirely by tuition.

The San Francisco School is a modified Montessori school for children ages three through twelve. The student body of 125 is middle class, integrated, and comes from all over the city. It was founded six years ago by a group of parents and is still controlled by the parents although they have turned the day-to-day operation of the school over to the staff. The school is located in a bright and spacious building inexpensively constructed with a lot of parent labor. It is supported by tuition and parent fundraising projects.

Berkeley High Community School is legally and physically part of the Berkeley public school system. It opened in January 1969 and presently has 225 students, selected by lottery from among Berkeley high school students who apply. Its racial and sex composition reflects the same proportions found in the population of Berkeley high school. The school is divided into four tribes, each of which has its own physical space and meets once or twice a week to decide operational questions and resolve interpersonal conflicts. General policy is set by an Inter-Tribal Council of students and staff. Each student is free to choose his or her courses or to develop new ones within the liberally interpreted requirements for high school graduation.

New Community School, in Oakland, California, sees itself as an active participant in the struggle for social justice. Its 50 high school age students, half of them white and half black, half low income and half middle income, come from the surrounding community of North

Oakland. The school takes stands on community issues and the curriculum is developed out of the perceived needs of the community as well as the skills individuals need in order to survive. The budget is raised partly from tuition and partly from foundation grants. It is governed by a board of directors comprised of students, staff, parents, and other community representatives.

Primary Life School is a parent controlled and operated school in San Francisco for four to eight year olds. There are about 30 students of mixed racial and economic backgrounds. A head teacher and assistant teacher provide continuity for the children and guidance for the parents. A rich environment coupled with a structure similar to British infant schools allows the child to pursue his interests freely without interfering with other students' activities. Tuition paid by parents provides the financial base for the school.

The Group School is an independent high school for working class white and Black youth from Cambridge. It was originated by students in 1970 and is presently governed by a community meeting and board, each of which is composed of more students than staff. The thirty-eight students range in age from 15 to 21 and participate in a non-graded program designed to teach basic skills, integrate employment into education, and provide for emotional and intellectual development in an atmosphere which is conscious of the history of the working class in America. A sliding scale tuition provides a small percentage of the school's budget, with the remainder coming from private and foundation support and government contracts.

The Highland Park Free School is a parent-controlled community school enrolling over 200 students between the ages of 5 and 14. The students, who are admitted on a first-come, first-served basis, are predominantly black and come from the Highland Park section of Roxbury. The curriculum is a mix of basic skills taught in small groups within each class and less formally structured, student-centered afternoon projects. Each class is run by a community teacher with the help of a professional teacher. The school charges no tuition and is supported through foundation grants and local fundraising activities. Highland Park is one of three Black community schools in the Federation of Boston Community Schools.

Michael Community School is a non-graded community school serving about 235 students ranging in age from 5 to 13. The school began when St. Michael's, a Catholic parochial school, was forced to close because of financial difficulties. The school is governed by a board elected from the neighborhood and stresses parent involvement in all phases of its governance. Though the school does lease its building from the church, it is no longer a Catholic school in its curriculum, staff, or form of decision-making. The student body is mixed Black, white, and Spanish-speaking. Michael Community School is one of seven members of the Milwaukee Federation of Community Schools, all of which were taken over by the community when the church could no longer support them.

The Ironbound Children's Center includes a preschool for 45 children ages three to four, the beginning of a primary school now enrolling 21 children ages 5 through 7 and an after school enrichment program for youngsters ages 6 through 12. All these are governed by a parent board. The center is the outgrowth of a series of parent meetings and seminars which discussed personal experiences with school and new methods of teaching. The classrooms are open structure, and have three teachers—a head teacher, an assistant teacher, and a parent. All have the same status within the class. Twenty-five percent of the students are Black and the remainder are mixed white ethnic including Spanish-speaking and Portuguese. All come from the Ironbound district of Newark, New Jersey. Funding comes from the State Department of Education, federal grants, private donations. There is no tuition.

Index